The
C-Suite Blind Spot

Executive Strategy for Search, AI, and Visibility Governance

Ash Nallawalla

https://www.linkedin.com/in/ashnallawalla

Keywords: C-Suite, Executive Leadership, Digital Strategy, Search Visibility, Organic Search, Corporate Governance, Digital Transformation, AI Search, Large Language Models, SEO Strategy, Digital Risk Management, Marketing ROI

658.4092 : Technology and Application of Knowledge > Management and Auxiliary Services > Management > Executive Leadership and Governance

BUS075000 BUSINESS & ECONOMICS / Leadership

BUS104000 BUSINESS & ECONOMICS / Corporate Governance

BUS043000 BUSINESS & ECONOMICS / Marketing / General

BUS090050 BUSINESS & ECONOMICS / E-Commerce / Search Engine Optimization

TABLE OF CONTENTS

PREFACE

Executives manage what they can see. Visibility has become one of the most valuable—and least visible—assets organizations depend on.

For decades, search engine optimization (SEO) operated quietly in the background. It rarely appeared on the board agenda, yet it influenced demand, margins, and growth at scale. Today, that blind spot has widened. Discovery is no longer mediated only by search engines, rankings, or websites. It is increasingly mediated by large language models, AI assistants, and automated systems that summarize, recommend, and interpret organizations on behalf of decision-makers.

Visibility now sits at the intersection of marketing, technology, governance, and artificial intelligence—and is more exposed than most leadership teams realize.

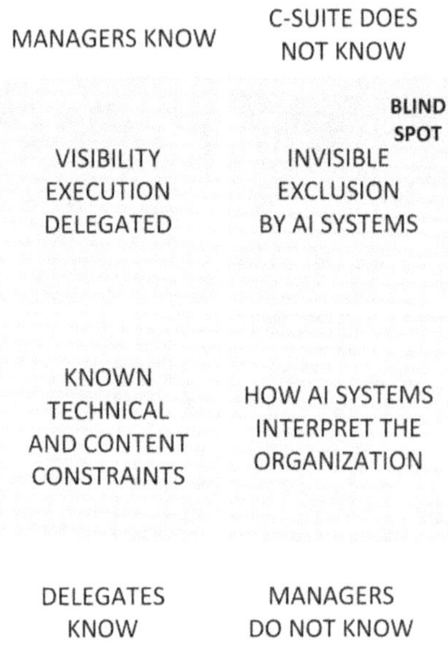

Figure 1 The Visibility Blind Spot in AI-Mediated Discovery

The Johari Window, a psychological model that illuminates what we know and what we fail to see, provides a useful analogy. Organizational visibility now occupies the most dangerous quadrant: unknown to leadership, yet material to outcomes. Revenue, trust, and consideration are increasingly shaped by systems executives do not directly observe, measure, or govern.

Every organization depends on being found. Yet in many boardrooms, discoverability still receives limited attention, even though it drives a substantial share of inbound demand across most industries. Historically, organic search visibility operated quietly—until it faltered and forced spending elsewhere. Today, the risk is more subtle. Visibility can erode, shift, or fragment without any obvious decline in traffic, leads, or reported performance.

This book exists to close that gap.

Most AI governance frameworks focus inward—on how organizations deploy technology, manage internal risk, and control automated decision-making. This book addresses a different exposure: how search engines, AI systems, and automated discovery platforms interpret, summarize, and represent your organization externally.

You can be compliant, ethical, and well governed internally—and still be misrepresented, deprioritized, or invisible to the systems that increasingly mediate customer choice. That external interpretability gap is rarely owned, measured, or governed. It is the blind spot this book addresses.

This book is for:

- Executives who need a clear connection between visibility, margin protection, and strategic resilience.
- Boards that require visibility governance integrated into financial oversight and risk management.

- Digital leaders who are building durable infrastructure rather than running disconnected campaigns.
- Agencies and consultants who are seeking language that elevates visibility from tactics to enterprise value.

Throughout this series, "SEO" refers to both the discipline and the practitioners—the people responsible for protecting discoverability, authority, and trust. In this volume, that responsibility is expanded to include visibility across AI-mediated surfaces, where influence increasingly occurs before attribution and outside traditional reporting systems.

THE COST OF INACTION

Customers have changed how they buy—and machines increasingly decide what they see first. They block push marketing, ignore unsolicited outreach, and curate their digital experiences. But they still search, ask, and consult automated systems. Every interaction is a self-qualified expression of demand. When your organization is missing, a competitor is being recommended instead.

Paid and organic discovery are not competing channels—they are interdependent. Traditional SEO quality still influences paid performance through relevance signals and Quality Scores. But AI-mediated visibility introduces a new layer: organizations can now influence decisions without receiving a visit, a click, or a measurable interaction. When visibility weakens, demand does not disappear. It is redirected—often silently—toward alternatives that automated systems can interpret with greater confidence.

Visibility

In executive terms, visibility is no longer just traffic acquisition. It is discoverability insurance—protection for how your organization is found, trusted, and chosen when machines mediate the decision process.

You insure facilities, finances, and data. Visibility governance insures your representation in search engines, AI summaries, assistants, and automated evaluations. When that coverage lapses, you pay the premium again through higher acquisition costs, lost consideration, and declining influence.

THE BUSINESS CASE FOR EXECUTIVE ATTENTION

Visibility maturity protects revenue already within reach. Structural friction, content inconsistency, and governance gaps erode discoverability—usually without detection. Small improvements in clarity, accessibility, performance, and authority scale across thousands of interactions each day, shaping perception long before sales or attribution systems engage.

In a world of tightening budgets and rising customer acquisition costs, governed visibility remains one of the most capital-efficient levers for profitable growth. The return compounds when it is treated as infrastructure rather than an activity.

WHY VISIBILITY OFTEN FEELS HARD

Most organizations inherit aging platforms, fragmented content systems, and unclear ownership. Discoverability is no longer a single-team responsibility; it relies on synchronized processes across product, engineering, UX, legal, analytics, communications, and now AI tooling. When leadership treats visibility as an isolated marketing function, progress resets with every restructure, platform change, or budget cycle.

RESPONSIBILITY WITHOUT GOVERNANCE IS RISK

Even when leaders acknowledge visibility's importance, the absence of clear governance leaves it exposed to:

- Fragmented decision-making
- Project timelines that cut structural corners
- Technology changes that silently degrade machine interpretability
- Restructures that remove institutional knowledge

Visibility is too important to depend on heroics.

HOW THIS BOOK IS USED

This book serves as supplementary material for the Visibility Governance Maturity Model VGMM)Workshop (covered in Book 3, AI Visibility Playbook). It establishes shared language, scope, and context before the workshop, ensuring participants approach governance questions from a common baseline. The workshop[1] is a facilitated executive session that produces a current-state governance determination. This book supports that process but does not replace the workshop or serve as an assessment, audit, or scoring tool.

HOW THIS BOOK FITS INTO THE SERIES

This is the fifth volume in the *Managing SEO* series—written from the leadership table, where strategy, finance, risk, and accountability converge.

---

[1] Inquire via crm911.com

- Book 1, *Managing SEO*, offers a concise overview for busy executives, linking governance, capability building, and visibility performance across digital channels.
- Book 2, *Accidental SEO Manager*, builds functional literacy and operational understanding.
- Book 3, *AI Visibility Playbook*, addresses automation, policy, and credibility protection.
- Book 4, *Is Our SEO Working?*, provides measurement and ROI frameworks.

Together, these volumes provide a blueprint for retaining discoverability as the digital ecosystem evolves.

IMPORTANT NOTICE TO READERS

This book presents frameworks, strategies, and governance approaches developed through the author's professional experience and industry observation. The content is intended for informational and educational purposes only.

This book does not provide:

- Legal advice or legal counsel
- Financial or investment advice
- Professional consulting services specific to your organization
- Recommendations tailored to your particular circumstances
- Guarantees of specific outcomes or results

What readers should understand:

Governance frameworks, regulatory requirements, and organizational best practices vary significantly across industries, jurisdictions, organizational sizes, and business models. What works for one organization may not be appropriate for another.

Before acting on information in this book:

- Consult qualified legal counsel regarding governance structures, compliance obligations, and regulatory requirements in your jurisdiction
- Engage financial advisors to evaluate budget allocations, investment decisions, and ROI projections
- Seek professional consulting services to adapt frameworks to your specific organizational context
- Review recommendations with internal stakeholders, including legal, compliance, risk management, and technical teams

Particularly critical areas requiring professional guidance:

- Legal compliance and regulatory obligations
- Board governance and fiduciary responsibilities
- Contract negotiations and vendor relationships
- Employee matters, including restructuring and talent management
- Financial reporting and audit requirements
- Data privacy and security obligations

The visibility governance landscape evolves continuously. Information current at publication may become outdated as regulations change, technologies evolve, and industry practices develop.

The author and publisher disclaim all liability for any decisions made, actions taken, or outcomes experienced based on information presented in this book. Readers assume full responsibility for evaluating the applicability of content to their specific situations and for seeking appropriate professional guidance.

WHAT COMES NEXT

Closing the visibility blind spot is not a technical task. It is a leadership mandate. When governance is strong, discoverability becomes predictable, costs become efficient, and decisions are guided by insight rather than assumption.

Your organization is already paying for visibility. This book will help ensure you stop paying rent for what you can govern, protect, and sustain.

– Melbourne, February 2026

Chapter 1

THE BLIND SPOT — WHY SEARCH VISIBILITY BELONGS IN THE BOARDROOM

EXECUTIVE SUMMARY

You depend on being found — but your visibility is governed by systems you probably never review. Most inbound digital revenue still comes from unpaid search, yet search engine optimization (SEO) receives only a fraction of the budget and almost no senior oversight. This gap between dependency and governance creates a structural risk that rarely appears on executive dashboards.

Across industries, more than half of all search demand is now satisfied without a website visit. Answers are delivered directly within search results, embedded inside applications, displayed on connected devices, incorporated into automated decision flows, and increasingly spoken aloud by digital assistants. Tens of billions of dollars in economic value now shift each year away from organizations that fund content and expertise toward platforms that reuse that material upstream— without appearing as traffic, leads, or conversions.

This chapter reframes search visibility as a **fiduciary** responsibility. When material revenue influence moves beyond measurable interaction, visibility becomes an asset that must be governed, measured differently, and protected with the same seriousness as financial or operational **infrastructure**.

THE BLIND SPOT: WHAT YOU CANNOT SEE IS COSTING YOU

Your organization is discoverable online — until it is not.

Executives can usually cite paid media spend with precision and forecast its near-term impact. Far fewer can state what share of inbound revenue originates from organic discovery, how sensitive that revenue is to visibility loss, or how quickly paid investment would need to increase to compensate. This **silence** creates a measurable but largely invisible exposure.

When organic visibility declines, demand rarely disappears. Instead, it is displaced. Paid channels expand quietly to preserve volume, masking the loss of owned discovery. Revenue appears stable. Margins erode. By the time financial pressure becomes visible, the underlying exposure has already compounded.

Ignoring search visibility does not remove the risk. It delays recognition until corrective action is more expensive and less effective.

THE COST OF THE INVISIBLE CHANNEL

Organic discovery has historically been your most efficient growth engine — but only when actively maintained.

When search capability matures, it compounds over time. When it stalls, the consequences are subtle at first. Revenue does not collapse. Instead, customer acquisition costs rise as paid channels are used to offset the decline in organic contribution. Performance reports remain acceptable. Traffic may even appear flat.

The cost emerges elsewhere. Profit shrinks. Budget dependency increases. Strategic flexibility disappears.

A common pattern clearly illustrates the issue. A modest decline in organic contribution forces a disproportionate increase in paid spend to maintain volume. The resulting profit shortfall often exceeds the entire investment required to prevent the decline in the first place. This is **visibility debt**. Like financial debt, it accrues interest when ignored and becomes costly to refinance under pressure.

Compounding the problem, not all visibility leaves a measurable trail. **Many modern systems now read, summarize, and reuse website content without requiring visitors to visit the site**. Traditional analytics record only what happens after a click, creating the illusion that nothing occurred when traffic does not appear.

In reality, organizations already maintain basic access records that capture every visit to their digital properties—by people and by automated systems alike. These records confirm that content is being accessed and processed by machines that influence decisions elsewhere, even when no session, lead, or conversion is recorded. For executives, this reinforces a blind spot: the absence of dashboard evidence does not mean there is no impact.

ZERO-CLICK SEARCH AND THE HIDDEN TRANSFER OF VALUE

Search visibility risk is no longer confined to ranking loss or traffic decline. An increasing share of customer decisions now occurs without a website visit.

Search engines and AI-driven interfaces increasingly deliver summaries, comparisons, and recommendations directly within their own environments. These responses appear in search results, within applications, across devices, and in automated workflows that guide choice. In these moments, your organization may influence a decision without being visited—or may be excluded entirely without realizing it.

This does not eliminate demand. It relocates where value is captured.

From an executive perspective, this represents a hidden transfer of economic value. The organization continues to fund expertise, content, and authority, yet **monetization increasingly occurs upstream inside platforms it does not control.** Influence remains real, but attribution weakens. Measurement lags. Governance remains anchored to an earlier model of discovery.

The exposure varies sharply by business model. Organizations dependent on early-stage education, high-value leads, or comparison-driven discovery carry materially greater risk than those relying primarily on branded navigation or late-stage transactions. Two companies can appear equally visible while facing very different revenue vulnerabilities.

A secondary effect further obscures the risk. As organic discovery delivers fewer measurable visits, paid acquisition is often expanded to compensate, even as paid efficiency declines. Costs rise to replace demand that still exists but no longer arrives through owned channels. Margins compress quietly, while reports remain deceptively calm.

For leadership, the issue is not whether zero-click visibility is "good" or "bad." Discoverability has moved earlier in the decision journey, outside traditional measurement boundaries, while financial accountability remains unchanged. When influence precedes attribution, optimization alone is insufficient. Governance determines whether visibility becomes a durable asset or a silent liability.

In practical terms, this means organizations may be evaluated, compared, or excluded by machines **without their websites ever being consulted.**

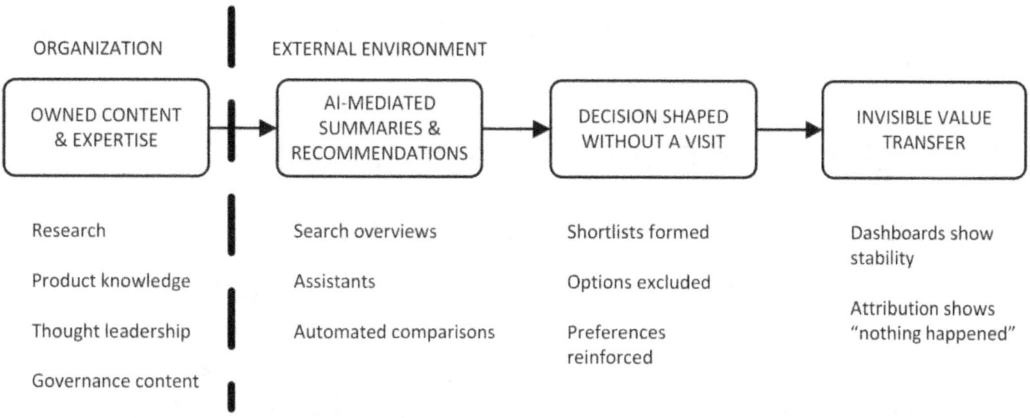

Figure 2 Zero-Click Value Transfer in AI-Mediated Discovery.

WHY LEADERS OVERLOOK IT

Visibility Appears Tactical

Search infrastructure often feels operational. Page structure, metadata, content hygiene, and system accessibility do not resemble traditional board-level concerns—until they determine how demand is summarized, redirected, or excluded by automated systems at scale.

Accountability Is Diffuse

- Marketing owns messaging.
- Technology owns platforms.
- Content owns production.
- No function owns outcome.

When responsibility is shared without ownership, governance fails by default.

The Results Are Not Immediate

Paid channels align neatly with quarterly cycles. Organic and AI-mediated visibility compounds over the years. Early deterioration is easy to ignore and difficult to justify interrupting short-term priorities to address. The governing rule is consistent: what nobody owns eventually breaks.

WHEN VISIBILITY BECOMES A FIDUCIARY ISSUE

Search visibility has become a **strategic infrastructure**.

AI-driven discovery systems reward organizations with clean structure, accessible content, validated trust signals, and consistent representation across digital surfaces. Those without these foundations are already disappearing from emerging interfaces, often without realizing it.

Market winners will be those whose visibility does not depend entirely on rented reach. When material revenue influence moves beyond attribution, dashboards, and formal oversight, the exposure is no longer marketing inefficiency. It becomes **AI-mediated visibility**—because executives remain accountable for outcomes they are no longer equipped to observe or govern.

THE LEADERSHIP MANDATE

What you choose to govern signals what the business values.

Your mandate is not to manage tactics, but to establish **accountability**. You must ensure that visibility—both SEO-driven and GEO-mediated—is treated as **infrastructure**, not as a discretionary marketing activity. You must assign ownership for organic and machine-mediated revenue exposure. You must demand reporting that distinguishes owned growth from rented reach.

Competitive advantage accrues to organizations whose executives make a deliberate decision:

"We will be found — reliably, efficiently, and everywhere our customers look."

Chapter 2

THE HIDDEN COST OF UNDER-FUNDING VISIBILITY

EXECUTIVE SUMMARY

Organic search accounts for a disproportionate share of high-margin inbound revenue for most organizations, yet it is routinely treated as a secondary priority. When investment in search capability stalls, rising paid acquisition costs quietly absorb the impact. Revenue appears stable. Margins deteriorate. The result is a financial liability that compounds without triggering traditional controls.

This chapter reframes search visibility as a capital investment rather than a marketing expense. It outlines how underfunding erodes profitability, why this erosion is difficult to detect in standard reporting, and which financial signals boards should monitor to prevent the silent erosion of shareholder value.

MARGIN EROSION AND EXECUTIVE CONTROL

You may be spending millions to acquire customers, but far less to protect the visibility that makes acquisition efficient.

When organic performance weakens, the impact is rarely immediate. Revenue does not track with visibility loss. Instead, paid channels expand to compensate. Media budgets rise gradually, often justified as "supporting growth," while the underlying cause remains unexamined. Profit disappears quietly inside higher acquisition costs.

This erosion does not appear as an explicit "SEO loss" in the profit and loss statement. It hides inside cost inflation. Over time, the organization begins paying repeatedly for demand it once captured without incremental spend. Visibility that was owned becomes visibility that must be rented.

THE HIDDEN ECONOMICS OF SEARCH

Paid and organic visibility operate under fundamentally different financial models.

Paid visibility is a variable cost (and it does nothing to improve your visibility to large language models.) Each incremental unit of demand requires incremental spend, and competition ensures that unit costs trend upward over time. When budgets pause, value disappears immediately.

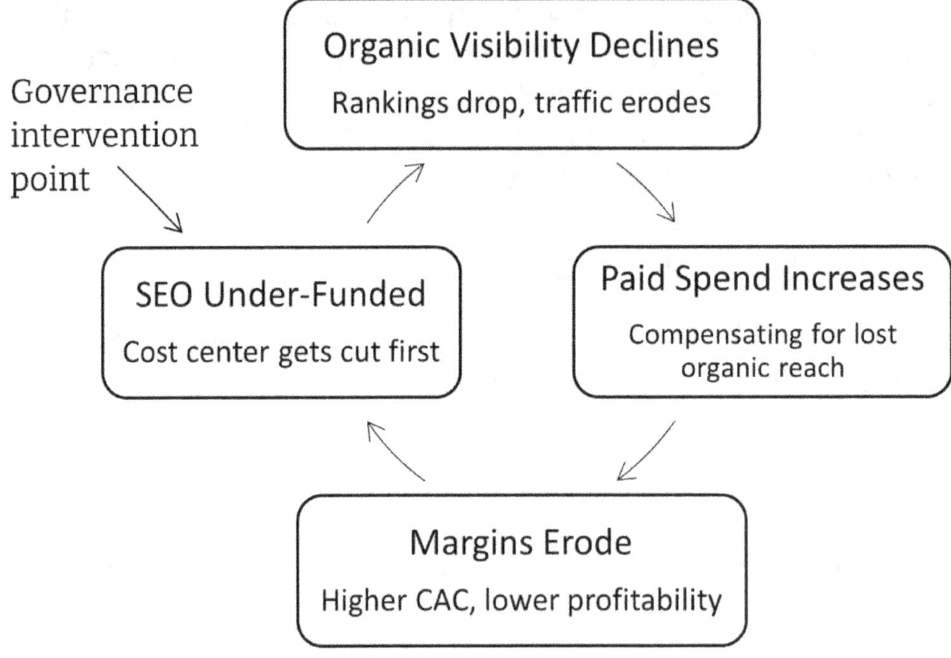

Figure 3 The Margin Erosion Cycle: How Under-Funding Creates Compounding Risk.

Organic visibility behaves like a capital asset. Once authority, relevance, and technical foundations are established, incremental discovery carries minimal marginal cost. The return compounds are provided that the asset is maintained.

A relatively small shift in the mix can have an outsized impact: even a 10% shift from organic to paid can cause customer acquisition costs to rise faster than most executives anticipate. EBITDA pressure appears not to be due to revenue decline, but to efficiency.

This is why visibility mix deserves the same scrutiny as channel mix in any capital allocation discussion.

WHY UNDER-FUNDING PERSISTS

Search capability is frequently misclassified as discretionary marketing spend. Funded episodically, it is expected to justify itself within short reporting cycles and is among the first areas to be reduced under budget pressure. This framing encourages tactical activity rather than sustained capability building.

Attribution further obscures the issue. Paid channels often receive credit for conversions that were initiated earlier through organic discovery, reinforcing the perception that paid investment is doing the heavy lifting. Meanwhile, the contribution of organic visibility remains under-reported and under-defended.

Complexity compounds the problem. Executives are comfortable with auction-based media models and cost-per-click dynamics. Crawling, indexing, and visibility decay feel abstract by comparison. What is poorly understood is rarely prioritized for funding.

The governing pattern is consistent: what is not measured becomes optional, and optional assets are eventually under-invested.

COMPOUNDING COST OF NEGLECT

Under-investment creates liabilities that grow with time rather than resolve themselves.

Deferred capability building results in permanent opportunity loss, not a delayed benefit. Authority gaps widen. Competitors strengthen their positions. Recovery requires more time, more capital, and more disruption than early maintenance would have.

The longer neglect persists, the more the organization relies on paid channels to maintain volume. This increases exposure to pricing volatility, compresses margin, and reduces strategic flexibility during downturns. By the time financial pressure becomes visible, corrective options are limited.

REFRAMING ROI FOR ORGANIC VISIBILITY

Boards should anchor the discussion around a single exposure question:

"If organic discovery disappeared tomorrow, how much of our digital revenue would disappear with it?"

The answer reveals dependency more clearly than any traffic chart. It reframes search from an activity to a risk surface.

This shift improves capital discipline. Instead of treating SEO as an operating expense to minimize, leadership views it as an asset with a compounding yield profile. When funded consistently, organic visibility often delivers returns that exceed most alternative growth investments after break-even, which typically occurs within 12 months, depending on competitive intensity.

GOVERNANCE TRIGGERS FOR EXECUTIVE OVERSIGHT

Executives should initiate escalation protocols when any of the following indicators emerge:

- **Organic market share declines by more than 10% year-over-year**
  Signals erosion in brand visibility and competitive positioning.
- **Paid media spend is increasing faster than revenue growth**
  Indicates declining acquisition efficiency and potential over-reliance on paid channels.
- **No performance review of organic search delivered within six months**
  Suggests a gap in oversight of a critical revenue and reputation channel.
- **Search visibility or indexation trends show sustained negative movement**
  Early warning of technical or strategic misalignment that may impact discoverability.

These indicators serve as early warning signs of digital risk. Escalating early enables proactive intervention before revenue or reputation is materially affected.

ACTION FRAMEWORK FOR SECURING PROFITABILITY

Use this sequence to expose the blind spot and rebalance investments:

- **Audit the mix**: Request a 24-month paid vs. organic performance view
- **Quantify exposure**: Model EBITDA impact of losing 30% of organic traffic

- **Fund the fix**: Reinvest a defined portion of paid-media savings into SEO maturity
- **Institutionalize governance**: Add organic visibility to quarterly performance reports

Executives do not need to understand every ranking factor — only whether the organization **is capturing or losing margin**.

The specific measurement frameworks, financial metrics, and dashboard structures for tracking the impact of visibility on margin and profitability are detailed in Chapter 7: **Measuring What Matters.** That chapter provides the executive reporting tools needed to operationalize the governance triggers and action framework outlined above.

BOARD TAKEAWAYS

- Organic visibility is the highest-margin revenue driver
- Under-funding forces rising dependence on paid acquisition
- The financial risks **increase silently** over time
- Balanced investment preserves profit and strategic agility
- Boards should treat search visibility like any other enterprise asset — governed, measured, and protected

Chapter 3
SEO AS STRATEGIC INFRASTRUCTURE

EXECUTIVE SUMMARY

Search visibility is not a campaign that can be switched on and off. It is **infrastructure** that must be built, maintained, and governed. When treated as a capital asset with shared ownership, automated enforcement, and clear accountability, visibility becomes predictable and resilient. When treated as tactical marketing, it becomes fragile, expensive, and vulnerable to organizational change.

This chapter explains how to govern discoverability with the same discipline applied to other mission-critical systems, ensuring it survives restructures, platform shifts, and leadership transitions.

INFRASTRUCTURE THINKING AT THE EXECUTIVE LEVEL

You already govern infrastructure. Availability, cybersecurity, data integrity, and compliance receive sustained investment because failure carries material risk.

Search visibility operates under the same logic. It influences revenue, cost efficiency, and brand trust at scale. Infrastructure thinking recognizes that capability must exist before urgency forces action, that systems require continuous maintenance, and that resilience matters more than short-term performance spikes.

CAMPAIGN THINKING VS. CAPABILITY THINKING

When SEO is funded episodically, performance fluctuates with spend. Knowledge departs with agencies or individuals. Gains must be repurchased repeatedly. Visibility becomes unpredictable and increasingly expensive to sustain.

Capability thinking embeds **discoverability** into how the organization operates. Governance is enforced through release cycles, quality gates, shared standards, and cross-functional accountability. Progress survives turnover. Improvement accumulates.

WHAT SEO AS INFRASTRUCTURE LOOKS LIKE

Governance as the Operating Layer

Strong infrastructure requires:

- Shared ownership — CMO + CTO + Finance + Risk
- Central quality standards — schema, taxonomy, accessibility
- Defined escalation paths when visibility is at risk

If everyone owns SEO, no one owns it.

Ownership must be explicit — not implied.

You may already be facing this without knowing it. Employees are quietly adopting their own AI tools—"Bring Your Own AI" (BYOAI)—to accelerate content creation, analysis, and decision-making. While the intent is productivity, the result is unsupervised automation that can shape how your organization appears online without governance approval.

Documented, Repeatable, Automated Processes

To remove friction and risk, establish:

- SEO and accessibility checks in the CMS

- Automated monitoring of Core Web Vitals and indexation
- Release pipelines that enforce discoverability

Automation ensures compliance without slowing teams.

Infrastructure for Machines, Not Just Humans

SEO infrastructure is no longer built solely for human discovery. Increasingly, it must support automated agents—search engines, AI assistants, procurement bots, recommendation systems, and internal copilots—that interpret your organization for decision-makers.

These systems do not browse websites the way people do. They extract meaning, compare entities, validate claims, and synthesize summaries across sources. If your infrastructure does not support that consumption model, your visibility degrades—even if your rankings appear stable.

From an executive perspective, this changes the meaning of "infrastructure readiness."

Modern visibility infrastructure must ensure:

- Core product, service, and policy information is machine-extractable
- Definitions and attributes are consistent across pages and systems
- Authoritative pages are stable, referenceable, and regularly maintained
- Structured data reinforces—not contradicts—visible content
- Critical information is not locked behind scripts, images, or gated flows

Organizations that fail here often misdiagnose the problem. They invest in more content, more campaigns, or more paid support—while the underlying infrastructure prevents AI systems from reliably interpreting that content.

This is why SEO belongs alongside platforms, data, and security in infrastructure discussions. Visibility systems now behave like upstream dependencies. When they break, downstream effects appear in sales efficiency, procurement friction, and brand trust—often without obvious attribution.

Executives who treat SEO as infrastructure fund it differently. They prioritize durability over novelty, clarity over volume, and governance over tactics. In doing so, they ensure their organization remains legible not just to customers, but also to the systems customers increasingly rely on to make decisions.

PLATFORM STANDARDIZATION AND OPERATING EFFICIENCY

Fragmented platforms dilute accountability and increase cost. Multiple content systems, inconsistent tagging, and conflicting analytics erode data integrity and decision confidence.

Standardization — a single analytics framework, approved tooling, and unified publishing architecture — reduces operational drag and strengthens governance.

PERFORMANCE AS A MANAGED METRIC

Visibility should be managed with the same rigor applied to other operational systems. Leaders should expect reporting on visibility equity, high-intent coverage, indexation health, schema completeness, and regression resolution time.

When executives ask consistently about performance, discipline follows.

PROTECTING VISIBILITY DURING CHANGE

Restructures Must Not Break Infrastructure

Reorganizations often disconnect teams who must collaborate to maintain rankings.

To safeguard performance:

- Ensure SEO owners are identified in all new org charts
- Maintain cross-functional visibility councils through transitions
- Protect "discoverability" capabilities from budget cuts

If no one is accountable during a restructure, visibility becomes collateral damage.

CMS Migrations and the "Content Disposal" Risk

When platforms change, teams often delete older pages to speed delivery. But removing historical content:

- Removes internal authority pathways
- Breaks backlinks and navigation context
- Lowers relevance for long-tail demand

Guidance for leaders:

- Ensure technical preservation measures are planned and funded before content removal
- Build time and budget buffers for content preservation
- Measure value before deleting pages — not after traffic collapses

Modern SEO resilience depends on continuity.

Capacity Building as Future-Proofing

Your infrastructure outlives individuals.

To avoid dependency on "hero experts":

- Maintain scalable best-practice libraries
- Cross-train product, content, and engineering teams
- Build internal career pathways for SEO skills
- Grow data science capability to support AI-driven visibility

Resilience is a staffing decision.

THE EXECUTIVE ROLE IN DIGITAL INFRASTRUCTURE MATURITY

You don't need to know how search engines work — you need to ask the questions that ensure your teams are accountable for visibility, performance, and compliance.

Key reports to request each quarter:

- **How many page templates meet performance and usability benchmarks?**
  A drop may signal user experience or discoverability issues.

- **What percentage of published pages meet compliance and content standards?**
  This reflects how well your digital footprint aligns with governance expectations.

- **What share of search-driven conversions comes from organic (unpaid) traffic?**
  A shrinking share may indicate over-reliance on paid media or a decline in authority.

- **How quickly are performance issues being resolved?**
  Lagging response times suggest operational risk or resource gaps.

- **Are teams meeting internal policy standards during audit cycles?**
  Declining scores indicate process breakdowns or training needs.

If any of these indicators trend downward, your visibility risk is rising — often before revenue impact is felt.

EXECUTIVE INSIGHT

The framing has changed.

Old view: SEO is a marketing initiative.

Current reality: SEO is enterprise infrastructure.

Campaigns create short-lived gains. Infrastructure creates sustained confidence. When discoverability is governed like any critical system, organizations reduce their reliance on paid services and maintain trust as platforms evolve.

Chapter 4

GOVERNANCE AND ACCOUNTABILITY ACROSS FUNCTIONS

EXECUTIVE SUMMARY

Search visibility only succeeds when everyone plays their role—Marketing, Product, IT, Legal, Risk, HR, and Communications. But without clear ownership, SEO becomes the first thing sacrificed when speed, politics, or priorities collide.

This chapter shows you how to design governance that keeps visibility reliable through:

- Distributed ownership with executive oversight
- Automated quality controls built into routine workflows
- Skills development that sustains capability through turnover
- Change-management guardrails that protect visibility during restructures and platform changes

When governance becomes part of culture—not a compliance exercise—discoverability remains strong even when budgets tighten, or systems transform.

WHY GOVERNANCE IS EVERYONE'S JOB

Search performance is never created by one department. It's the culmination of how your organization writes, codes, designs, approves, and maintains content.

You don't need a new committee. You need clarity:

- Who owns visibility-impacting decisions?
- When does Legal review apply?
- Who escalates risk before traffic drops?
- How do AI-assisted outputs get validated?

Governance ensures synchronization across functions — so no team accidentally breaks what another team built.

WHEN THE SYSTEM FAILS, SEO FAILS — EVEN WHEN THE TEAM DOESN'T

Most SEO failures aren't executional. They're structural.

You can have a high-performing team — skilled, motivated, aligned — and still watch performance erode when:

- Publishing pipelines block indexation
- CMS releases bypass compliance safeguards
- Governance pauses under shifting priorities
- AI content outpaces validation capacity
- Template changes silently strip schema or accessibility

These aren't edge cases. They're systemic vulnerabilities. And when visibility drops, the blame often falls on the SEO team—not on the infrastructure that made success unsustainable.

Here's the leadership test:

"If every SEO task were completed flawlessly this month, would the system allow the results to stick?"

If the answer is no, you don't have a talent problem. You have a system problem.

Governance exists to make the system safe by default — so outcomes depend less on heroics and more on structure.

But here's the tension:

When pressure to maintain or raise the stock price intensifies, boards often set aside governance principles in favor of short-term optics.

That's when visibility risk compounds quietly — until it shows up in revenue.

Your role isn't just to request better reporting. It's to ensure the system can maintain performance—even under pressure.

Blind-Spot Check

If SEO success depends on individuals pushing uphill, capability will vanish when they do.

DISTRIBUTED OWNERSHIP WITH CENTRALIZED STEERING

Governance works when the people doing the work own the quality — and when executives own alignment.

Typical accountability model:

Function	Ownership Contribution
Marketing	Messaging, relevance, and content governance
Product	Prioritization tied to business outcomes
IT & Engineering	Accessibility, speed, architecture, and releases
Legal & Compliance	Risk, accuracy, regulatory alignment

Function	Ownership Contribution
CHRO / Talent Leadership	Skills, capability, resilience, and organizational design
C-Suite	Funding, prioritization, escalation

Data governance also plays a critical role by ensuring the accuracy, consistency, and accessibility of the data signals that search engines and AI systems rely on to represent your business.

Your role is to make visibility a **shared priority** — not a siloed responsibility.

EMBEDDING GUARDRAILS INTO WORKFLOWS

Governance fails if dependent on heroics. It succeeds when embedded in tools and processes.

Recommended controls:

- Pre-launch checks for SEO, accessibility, schema
- Release gates preventing SEO-breaking deployments
- Automated monitoring of speed and indexing
- Oversight of **AI-generated** content before publishing

Automation reduces friction — and removes excuses.

Accountability for Machine-Mediated Representation

Search visibility is no longer limited to pages your teams publish or campaigns your marketers run. Increasingly, it is shaped by machine-mediated representations—**summaries, comparisons, and recommendations generated by AI systems outside your direct control.** These representations influence customer decisions, partner confidence, and regulatory perception, often without producing a click or an audit trail.

This creates a governance problem that many organizations have not yet named: **when AI systems mischaracterize your organization, no executive role is clearly accountable for the outcome**.

Marketing may argue that AI summaries are "not our content."
Legal may argue that no formal publication occurred.
Technology may argue that the systems are external.

The result is a visibility gap with no owner.

From a governance perspective, this is not a search issue—it is a **decision-rights failure**. Boards already expect named accountability for financial disclosures, cybersecurity posture, privacy compliance, and public statements. Machine-mediated representations now sit in the same risk category. They shape how your organization is understood at scale, but they are rarely assigned an executive steward.

This gap matters because AI-generated summaries can introduce material risk:

- Product capabilities may be overstated or mischaracterized.
- Compliance or safety constraints may be omitted.
- Outdated or partial information may be presented as a current fact.
- Competitive positioning may be reframed unfavorably without rebuttal.

When these outcomes occur, the question executives must answer is simple: **Who is responsible for detecting, correcting, and preventing recurrence?**

Effective governance treats AI visibility as a shared but accountable domain. While execution spans Marketing, Technology, Legal, and

Product, **ultimate responsibility must be explicit**, with escalation paths defined before an incident occurs. Without that clarity, organizations respond reactively—after reputational or commercial damage has already been done.

The managerial implication is clear: if your governance framework assigns ownership only to what you publish directly, you are exposed to what machines say on your behalf. Visibility without accountability is no longer a marketing risk; it is an executive one.

CHANGE-MANAGEMENT GOVERNANCE: ORGANIZATIONAL CONTINUITY

Change governance has two dimensions: organizational continuity (covered here) and technical process controls (covered in Chapter 6). This section addresses how to maintain visibility capability through restructures, team changes, and leadership transitions. Visibility doesn't disappear from dashboards — it disappears inside workflows.

Three high-risk scenarios for the board to question:

1. CMS Replacement

Teams under delivery pressure may cut:

- Redirects
- Template parity
- Legacy content that still earns authority

A caution for leaders: Low-traffic pages can still significantly contribute to overall site performance and value.

2. Reorgs and Team Fragmentation

When reporting lines shift, visibility often loses a champion.

- Key knowledge walks out during restructures

- No one notices until traffic declines

Require capability retention plans before org changes hit go.

3. Template Redesign or Content Migration

Design enhancements may break:

- Structured data
- Internal linking
- Navigation logic

Governance must enforce preservation before innovation.

HUMAN CAPABILITY AS A GOVERNANCE ASSET

Technology does not protect visibility — **people do**.

HR must be part of SEO governance:

- Talent mapping: Who knows what? Where are the gaps?
- Competency planning: SEO, analytics, accessibility, **data science**
- Cross-training: So, the departure of one person doesn't erase expertise
- Career paths: So, SEO isn't seen as a dead-end role

Invest in skillsets that anticipate where SEO is headed, not only where it has been.

Skills increasingly required:

- Structured data + schema strategy
- Content quality evaluation (E-E-A-T)
- Machine-learning assisted analytics
- Prompting & review skills for AI content generation

Governance maturity increases as talent resilience increases. Chapter 5 covers detailed resilience-building measures and the relationship between automation and human expertise.

MEASUREMENT AND ACCOUNTABILITY ENFORCEMENT

Governance only matters if someone is held accountable for it.

Ask for a quarterly report showing:

- Compliance with SEO publishing standards
- Technical health and risk indicators
- Velocity + quality of content updates
- Resolved vs. outstanding regressions
- AI-generated content oversight metrics

EXTERNAL VALIDATION: YOUR DIGITAL AUDIT FUNCTION

Independent reviews by a consultant provide:

- Credibility with boards/regulators
- Risk detection before headlines expose it
- Proof that governance is applied, not assumed

SUSTAINING CAPABILITY THROUGH PEOPLE, STRUCTURES, AND CHANGE

Visibility infrastructure only works if the organization retains the skills and stability to protect it. Technology supports SEO, but humans ensure its integrity.

CHRO as a Visibility Capability Partner

What HR needs from you:

- Role clarity — what good SEO capability looks like at your maturity level
- Recognition that visibility is a business-critical function, not optional resourcing
- Hiring profiles that include hybrid skill sets:
    - Product + content literacy
    - Basic data science and analytics familiarity
    - Governance discipline and cross-functional communication

SEO maturity correlates with **expertise retention**. Talent flight leads to:

- Lost institutional knowledge
- Re-learning already solved problems
- Regression in technical SEO and governance discipline

Hiring and development should be guided by a visibility competency model — one lives in Book 2, *Accidental SEO Manager*, and can be adapted to your scale.

Red Flag

Attrition in SEO roles rarely shows up in board reporting — but it silently affects revenue.

Restructure Without Regression

Reorganizations are usually designed to improve customer outcomes... yet they often break the systems that help customers find you.

Common restructure risk patterns:

- SEO specialists are scattered across teams with diluted influence
- New reporting lines that remove visibility from leadership conversations

The C-Suite Blind Spot

- Tool ownership changes that break access controls and automation workflows

To prevent regression:

- Maintain a central governance anchor (Center of Excellence or equivalent)
- Retain enterprise-level KPI ownership for visibility equity
- Treat roles that protect discoverability as continuity positions — not easily removed in workforce changes

Red Flag

If visibility risk isn't considered during restructures, infrastructure maturity will slide backward faster than it was built.

Content and CMS Migrations

CMS replacements are inflection points for ranking volatility.

Temptations that must be resisted:

- Removing "low-traffic" pages to meet project deadlines
- Launching without redirects for every relevant legacy URL
- Breaking internal link structures that maintain authority
- Omitting structured data because templates aren't ready

Those "unimportant" pages often:

- Carry backlink equity
- Support ranking clusters
- Enable navigation and crawl depth

Priorities for leaders:

- Count pages before and after migration — gaps reveal revenue risks

- Fund buffer resources for content transformation — not just new pages
- Require migration SEO sign-off as a non-negotiable go-live condition

Red Flag

Content removal is easy. Recovering lost authority is expensive — and sometimes impossible.

Capacity Building as Risk Insurance

Capability must rise with complexity.

Executives should sponsor:

- Quarterly cross-training between product, content, UX, and SEO
- Governance drills — "What happens if this breaks?"
- Scenario testing for algorithmic or platform disruptions
- Job shadowing so teams understand upstream and downstream dependencies

Signals of maturity:

- Fewer emergency escalations
- Faster recovery from ranking regressions
- Independent issue detection by non-SEO functions

Your objective: **visibility resilience** — the ability to remain findable when teams change, technology shifts, or the environment disrupts.

When capability is institutionally owned rather than individually held, restructures, staff turnover, or agency changes no longer threaten discoverability.

EXECUTIVE CHECKLIST FOR GOVERNANCE ALIGNMENT

- ☐ Governance appears on your leadership agenda at least twice a year
- ☐ CMO, CTO, CRO, and CHRO share accountability
- ☐ AI governance and visibility governance are formally linked
- ☐ CMS launches include visibility safeguards, redirects, and content retention plans
- ☐ Automation is approved, tracked, and supervised
- ☐ Governance KPIs exist — and inform compensation
- ☐ Cross-training is funded, and skills are mapped
- ☐ Internal escalation avoids "unknown ownership" delays

Strong governance prevents surprises. Silent failures become visible — early enough to fix.

Chapter 5

AI AND AUTOMATION — NEW GOVERNANCE IMPERATIVES

EXECUTIVE SUMMARY

Artificial intelligence and automation now influence how your business is represented, found, and trusted. Governance discussions often focus on AI ethics, privacy, and risk — but rarely on discoverability and brand accuracy.

This chapter shows you how to protect revenue, reputation, and visibility in a world where **machines increasingly decide what customers see first**.

Your leadership ensures automation amplifies trust, not neglect.

WHEN BRAND BECOMES A MACHINE PROPERTY

Executives are accustomed to treating the brand as a human perception problem. Messaging shapes perception. Advertising reinforces identity. Reputation emerges from experience. That model still matters—but it is no longer sufficient.

In AI-mediated discovery, **brand** is increasingly **computed** rather than perceived.

Before a customer encounters your website, an AI system may already have evaluated your credibility, relevance, and suitability. That evaluation is not emotional. It is probabilistic. Models synthesize signals across content consistency, corroboration, technical accessibility, and comparative clarity. The outcome is a decision about whether your organization is safe to recommend, summarize, or exclude.

This creates a new category of executive risk. A company can remain compliant, technically sound, and well-ranked in traditional search while being quietly omitted from AI-generated answers. No alert fires. No traffic cliff appears. Influence shifts elsewhere. This is visibility drift, and it often occurs without any obvious operational failure.

From a governance perspective, this means brand integrity is no longer governed only through marketing oversight. It is governed through **signal stewardship**. If internal systems publish conflicting definitions, outdated claims, or ambiguous positioning, AI systems respond conservatively by reducing reuse. Competitors with slower pipelines but tighter coherence gain advantage.

This is why visibility governance must extend beyond campaigns and into executive control frameworks. Leadership does not need to manage SEO execution, but it must own the conditions under which machines are allowed to interpret and reuse the organization's information. When automation accelerates output without governance, it amplifies inconsistency faster than humans can detect it.

The executive implication is clear. Brand risk is no longer limited to what customers think after they arrive. It now includes how machines describe the organization before a customer ever has the chance. Governing that interpretation is not a technical preference. It is a leadership responsibility.

When a brand becomes a machine property, visibility governance becomes an enterprise discipline.

PERSONAL INTELLIGENCE AND MARKET NARRATIVE COLLAPSE

Search visibility is no longer shaped solely by query intent, location, or device context. The individual increasingly shapes it.

Modern AI-mediated discovery systems increasingly generate answers outside a neutral, shared result set, particularly where personal context is explicitly available and permitted. These systems synthesize responses at inference time using a combination of indexed information and personal context signals derived from user behavior, preferences, history, and connected data environments. Two executives asking the same question may receive materially different guidance on the same organization, product, or risk—without either realizing that their views are individualized or incomplete.

While this personalization is currently most visible in assistant-led experiences rather than every traditional search interaction, the architectural shift is decisive: inference is no longer isolated from identity.

This represents a structural change in how markets perceive organizations.

Historically, search has served as a common reference point. While rankings varied, organizations could reasonably assume that customers, partners, regulators, and analysts were exposed to broadly similar information. That assumption no longer holds. AI systems now act as personalized briefing agents, filtering and prioritizing information based on what the system infers about the individual user rather than what the organization intends to communicate.

From a governance perspective, this erodes the concept of a single, stable market narrative.

Your organization no longer has a single, stable search presence. It has many parallel representations—each assembled dynamically, shaped by prior context, and capable of influencing decisions before any direct interaction. Visibility becomes fragmented, probabilistic, and asymmetric. Influence may be exerted without attribution, audit trails, or executive visibility.

This is not a marketing personalization issue. It is an interpretive exposure issue.

When AI systems personalize responses, they also personalize trust. Recommendations increasingly favor sources that align with a user's historical preferences, prior interactions, and inferred values. Organizations that lack consistent, credible signals across the broader digital ecosystem risk being filtered out—not because they are irrelevant, but because the system cannot confidently align them with the user's personal context.

The governance implication is immediate. Executives can no longer assume that approval of messaging, content strategy, or brand positioning results in a coherent external perception. The system that interprets and relays that information operates independently, drawing on signals accumulated over time and across platforms that leadership does not directly control.

This creates a new class of exposure: **interpretive drift**.

Interpretive drift occurs when an organization's intended positioning diverges from how automated systems describe it across personalized contexts. The drift is rarely visible in dashboards. It does not trigger alerts. It surfaces indirectly—through lost consideration, unexplained sales friction, higher acquisition costs, or declining trust in competitive evaluations where the organization appears misaligned, outdated, or absent.

Governing visibility in this environment requires a shift in executive thinking. The objective is no longer to optimize for a single ranking or even for inclusion in a generic answer layer. The objective is to maximize eligibility for accurate representation across diverse personal contexts while minimizing the risk of exclusion, mischaracterization, or silent deprioritization.

This elevates visibility governance from a performance discipline to a leadership responsibility. When machines brief individuals differently about the same organization, the risk is not inconsistency—it is invisibility in the moments that matter most.

AUTOMATION WITHOUT OVERSIGHT CREATES INVISIBLE LIABILITY

Executives often assume SEO performance is self-maintaining once delegated. In reality, unmonitored automation widens the very gap their inattention created.

Tools adopted to "save time" in publishing, content optimization, or reporting frequently alter search signals without review, undoing years of investment in brand visibility.

1. Data Exposure

Staff increasingly use generative tools to draft copy, meta descriptions, or internal summaries.

When they include live campaign data or unreleased material in prompts, that information leaves corporate control and may later resurface in outputs visible to competitors.

An unreviewed SEO-automation plugin can leak strategy as surely as a misplaced RFP. Samsung was embarrassed when its staff uploaded confidential information to ChatGPT.

2. Content Drift

AI rewrites of existing text often introduce factual drift — obsolete pricing, incorrect product attributes, or duplicate phrasing.

Executives who treat SEO as a "set-and-forget" line item rarely notice until rankings and conversions slide.

Brand reputation is quietly damaged not by bad intent but by neglectful oversight.

3. Volume Without Review

Departments chasing efficiency may auto-generate pages or category descriptions at scale. Search engines now detect and suppress such uniform material. The company believes it is expanding its reach; in practice, automation without editorial ownership erases visibility.

This is the modern version of unmeasured spend — marketing output with negative ROI.

4. Compliance Breaches

Accessibility and disclosure obligations extend to automated SEO content.

If AI-generated material fails to meet WCAG 2.2 Level AA or advertising standards, accountability lies with the company, not the vendor. Executives who never integrated SEO into governance discover, too late, that "marketing compliance" was an undefined territory.

5. Governance Implications

Unsupervised SEO automation converts an operational risk into a board-level liability. When leadership shows no curiosity about *how* automation modifies brand signals, oversight collapses into silence.

This is precisely the C-Suite blind spot: assuming visibility is a technical concern when, in fact, it is a reputational one.

Warning

If the board never asks whether automation affects search visibility or compliance, it has already accepted invisible risk.

Visibility Risk Is Now a Machine Decision, Not a Marketing Outcome

Automation changes how visibility risk materializes. In traditional search, visibility loss usually followed human decisions—content changes, technical failures, or competitive displacement that teams could observe and correct. In AI-mediated discovery, visibility can disappear without a triggering event you control or even see.

AI systems synthesize information across sources and make probabilistic judgments about what is safe, accurate, and worth presenting. When automation accelerates publishing, personalization, or content generation without governance, it increases the likelihood of subtle inconsistency: conflicting definitions, outdated claims, mismatched entity signals, or unsupported assertions. These inconsistencies rarely cause immediate penalties. Instead, they reduce confidence at the model level.

For executives, this creates a new category of risk. Your brand may remain compliant, technically sound, and well ranked in traditional search—while being quietly excluded from AI-generated answers, summaries, and recommendations. No alert fires. No traffic cliff appears. Influence shifts elsewhere.

This is why automation and visibility must be governed together. Automation increases speed and scale; governance preserves interpretability and trust. Without shared oversight, automated systems optimize for output while AI discovery systems optimize for certainty—and certainty favors competitors whose signals remain stable.

The executive task is not to slow automation, but to bound it. Governance must define where automation is permitted, where human review is mandatory, and how consistency is enforced across systems. Visibility risk is no longer confined to marketing performance. It is an enterprise exposure created when machines, not people, decide who is credible enough to be shown.

GUARDRAILS THAT PROTECT REPUTATION AND REVENUE

Strong SEO governance is not tactical management; it is a system of internal controls. Every executive understands financial audit; few apply that discipline to digital visibility. These guardrails convert a passive SEO budget into an accountable infrastructure.

1. Approved Tool Lists and Data Permissions

Every AI or SEO automation tool that touches customer or content data must be inventoried and risk-scored. Without this, marketing spends freely on opaque systems that rewrite site elements or metadata without traceability. Tool governance keeps ownership—and accountability—within the organization.

2. Review Checkpoints for Visibility-Affecting Changes

Any automation, including AI, that modifies title tags, schema, internal links, or copy must undergo human review. Executives should expect the same assurance here as in financial reporting: that there are *no unauthorized changes to material assets*. Search visibility is an intangible asset; altering it unreviewed is equivalent to adjusting revenue figures without an audit.

3. Human Accountability

Each automated workflow must name a responsible owner with the authority to halt or correct errors. When SEO sits too low in the hierarchy, accountability disappears. The C-Suite's role is to ensure ownership exists above the operational layer — not buried within it.

4. Quarterly Audits of Visibility Health

Boards routinely review cybersecurity posture; visibility deserves equal cadence. Audits should track ranking stability, structured-data integrity, and competitive share of voice. Without such a review, the company cannot determine whether automation is strengthening or weakening its strengths.

5. Escalation Paths for Visibility Incidents

When an automation error deletes pages or corrupts tracking, minutes matter. A predefined escalation route — marketing, IT, compliance, and executive sponsor — reduces downtime and protects revenue continuity. Without it, the brand's discoverability remains hostage to informal communication.

Implementation Notes

Executives need only three dashboard metrics to confirm SEO governance maturity:

1. Percentage of automated changes reviewed pre-deployment.

2. Time from visibility incident to executive notification.

3. Correlation between automation adoption and organic-traffic variance.

These reveal whether oversight exists or the blind spot persists. These **governance** oversight metrics are distinct from the **operational** performance metrics (NSM and supporting KPIs) detailed in Book 3, *Chapter 4 of the AI Visibility Playbook*. Executives need both: operational dashboards that show whether SEO is delivering results, and governance metrics that confirm the organizational capability to sustain those results.

Warning

If SEO governance never appears in risk or audit discussions, the company is effectively un-audited in one of its largest digital cost centers.

Server log files remain one of the few ways organizations can independently verify how automated systems interact with their digital assets. While analytics platforms report human behavior, log files record machine behavior—showing when search engine crawlers or AI-related bots request pages, how frequently they do so, and which sections of a site they access or ignore. For executives, the value of log data is not tactical optimization but governance assurance: confirming that visibility-critical systems can reach authoritative content, that unintended blocking has not occurred, and that AI or search exposure assumptions are grounded in observable evidence rather than inference alone.

Automation Magnifies Signal Drift Before Humans Notice It

Automation does not introduce new risks so much as it amplifies existing ones. When content creation, metadata generation, internal linking, personalization, or summarization become automated, small inconsistencies scale rapidly. A definition updated in one system but not another, a product claim altered in generated copy, or an outdated attribute carried forward by automation can fragment your meaning across the ecosystem.

Human reviewers often miss this drift because outputs still look "reasonable." Pages publish correctly. Analytics function. Rankings may even hold temporarily. But AI discovery systems detect divergence earlier than people do. When models encounter conflicting signals, they respond conservatively by reducing reuse. Visibility erosion begins long before any operational alarm is triggered.

From a governance perspective, this reframes automation risk. The primary failure mode is not a catastrophic error; it is a gradual loss of interpretability. Over time, your content becomes harder for machines to summarize confidently, compare accurately, or recommend safely. Competitors with slower pipelines but tighter governance gain an advantage—not because they innovate faster, but because their signals remain coherent.

Executives should treat automation as a force multiplier for both discipline and disorder. Where governance is strong, automation reinforces consistency and accelerates advantage. Where governance is weak, automation compounds ambiguity, reducing visibility and attribution.

The control point is not individual tools. It is signal stewardship. Governance must ensure that automated systems inherit the same definitions, constraints, review thresholds, and accountability structures as human-led work. Otherwise, automation quietly converts operational speed into strategic fragility.

AI Outputs Become De Facto Policy Without Oversight

When AI systems generate summaries, recommendations, explanations, or comparisons, their outputs quickly take on the authority of policy—whether you intended that or not. Internally, staff reuse AI-generated text in decks, briefs, and documentation. Externally, AI assistants paraphrase your content for customers, partners, and regulators. In both cases, the model's interpretation becomes the "official" version of your position.

This creates a subtle governance risk. If no one owns the accuracy, tone, and scope of AI outputs, the organization begins to operate on machine-generated interpretations rather than approved statements. Over time, this erodes message control. What the company *means* and what AI systems *say* about the company can diverge without any formal change process.

For executives, the issue is not whether AI is "right" in a technical sense. **It is whether AI outputs are authorized**. Policies, claims, compliance statements, and positioning must remain anchored to approved sources of truth. Governance must define which content is eligible for reuse, which outputs require review, and which topics are entirely off-limits to automation.

This is especially critical in regulated, safety-sensitive, or trust-dependent sectors. An AI summary that slightly overstates capability, simplifies a disclaimer, or blends multiple documents into a confident narrative can expose the organization to reputational or legal risk—even if no human intended to publish that claim.

Effective governance treats AI outputs as drafts, not decisions. It establishes clear escalation paths for high-risk topics and makes accountability explicit: someone owns the model inputs, someone owns the approval criteria, and someone monitors downstream use. Without this structure, AI quietly becomes an unaccountable policy engine—one that speaks often, confidently, and without memory of what it said yesterday.

Visibility Drift Accelerates Under Automation

Automation increases speed, scale, and consistency—but it also accelerates drift. Small inaccuracies, outdated assumptions, or imprecise definitions propagate faster when AI systems generate, summarize, and reuse content across channels. What once took months to spread through teams can now happen in days.

This creates a new executive risk pattern. Visibility does not usually collapse through a single failure. It erodes through accumulated micro-errors: an outdated product description reused by an assistant, an obsolete pricing qualifier summarized without context, or an old policy paraphrased as current guidance. Individually, these seem trivial. Collectively, they distort how markets, customers, and partners understand the organization.

Automation magnifies whatever governance already exists. Strong governance produces consistency at scale. Weak governance produces confident inconsistency at scale. Leaders should assume that any ambiguity in source material will be amplified, not corrected, by AI systems.

The executive implication is straightforward: drift detection must become a governed activity. It is no longer sufficient to review primary pages or flagship documents on a fixed cadence. Organizations need explicit checkpoints that test how AI systems currently describe the brand, its products, and its obligations. These checks reveal divergence early—before it hardens into reputation, expectations, or contractual misunderstandings.

This is not about policing every output. It is about establishing tolerances. Governance defines what "close enough" looks like, which deviations trigger review, and which topics demand zero variance. Without these thresholds, leaders discover visibility problems only after customers act on them.

Automation does not remove the need for judgment. It raises the cost of missing it.

WHY AUTOMATION CHANGES HOW YOU GET FOUND

Executives once assumed that if their brand had a website and an SEO budget, they were findable. That assumption no longer holds.

AI-driven automation and "machine customers" (Agentic search) now decide what people see before they ever reach your site.

Ignoring SEO governance in this environment means surrendering control of how your business is represented in the systems that guide purchasing and decision-making.

Automation Has Rewritten the Discovery Funnel

Search is no longer a human process that begins with a typed query and ends with a click.

Generative AI assistants, voice interfaces, and recommendation engines evaluate options before a person even sees them.

These systems extract and rank brand information directly from structured data, reviews, pricing pages, and product feeds.

If your visibility infrastructure is weak, your brand is filtered out long before the human decision point.

Executives who don't track how automation interprets their brand are effectively invisible to the new layer of search — the one customers never see, but that decides what they do.

Governance Check

If visibility reports track only traditional search rankings, you're auditing yesterday's discovery model.

Machine Interpretation Replaces Human Context

Automation reads content without nuance.

It doesn't understand brand promise, positioning, or pricing intent — only the signals encoded through structured data and technical consistency.

A single schema error or a conflicting product detail can cause a large language model or shopping feed to omit your offering entirely.

This is how under-investment in SEO infrastructure becomes a direct revenue leak.

Executives routinely fund brand advertising to shape perception; they rarely fund the structured accuracy that shapes algorithmic interpretation.

Both now determine reputation — one for humans, the other for machines.

The Compression of Time and Opportunity

AI systems compress the traditional buying journey into milliseconds:

$$\text{intent} \rightarrow \text{automated evaluation} \rightarrow \text{outcome}.$$

There is no window for mid-funnel persuasion when automation makes the decision.

If your visibility signals aren't aligned with that instantaneous evaluation, the opportunity is lost before the campaign even begins.

In this new environment, SEO governance is not about keyword strategy; it's about machine readiness.

Funding the Machine-Readable Brand

Automation favors brands with accurate, current, and complete data. That requires sustained investment in technical SEO, structured-data maintenance, and content verification.

These are not marketing tasks — they are infrastructure disciplines. Executives who treat them as optional create systemic exposure: brand data that's stale, inconsistent, or ignored by AI agents.

Budget stability ensures continuous verification of the brand's digital truth. Without it, automation fills gaps with whatever data it can find — often from competitors or outdated sources.

The Governance Imperative

Automation doesn't remove the need for leadership judgment; it removes the margin for error. AI can scale performance, but it scales neglect faster.

Executives who delegate SEO without oversight are allowing algorithms to write their external narrative. Governance reclaims control by enforcing accountability for the information systems that describe the business.

Governance Check

If no one in the company is accountable for how AI systems summarize your brand, the market will define it for you.

Summary

Automation has collapsed the discovery process into data interpretation.

When SEO is ignored or underfunded, automation interprets that silence as irrelevance.

Visibility governance must now serve as the company's data-defense system — the only barrier between the brand's intent and how machines present it to the world.

Automation Changes Accountability, Not Responsibility

Automation shifts *how* work is done, but it does not shift *who* is accountable. This distinction is frequently misunderstood at the executive level—and it creates exposure.

When AI systems generate content, summaries, recommendations, or classifications, responsibility does not transfer to the tool, the vendor, or the model. Accountability remains with the organization that deploys the system and benefits from its outputs. Regulators, courts, customers, and partners will always look upstream—to governance, not tooling.

This matters because automation often blurs ownership. **A generated answer may pass through marketing, product, legal, and IT systems without any one team recognizing it as "theirs."** When no one owns the output, no one governs its accuracy, tone, or implications. Over time, this creates unmanaged risk disguised as operational efficiency.

Executives must therefore govern *decision provenance*. For any automated or AI-assisted output that influences customers, regulators, or revenue, leadership should be able to answer three questions:

- Who approved the source material this output is based on?
- Who owns accuracy when the output is reused or summarized?
- Who is accountable when the output causes harm, confusion, or loss?

Without clear answers, automation introduces invisible liability. With clear answers, automation becomes a controlled multiplier of organizational capability.

The practical implication is simple: governance models must map accountability to outcomes, not tools. AI does not need permission—but it does need ownership. When leadership makes that explicit, automation strengthens trust instead of eroding it.

EXECUTIVE ROLE IN CAPABILITY RESILIENCE

Automation can execute processes, but it cannot govern them. Executives who believe automation reduces their dependence on skilled staff misunderstand both SEO and AI.

Every automated system still depends on human expertise to design, verify, and correct its decisions. When SEO is underfunded or misclassified as a technical afterthought, automation magnifies that weakness rather than fixing it.

Automation Increases, Not Reduces, Human Dependency

Generative tools can draft copy, summarize analytics, or flag technical issues, but they cannot decide what information is correct, ethical, or strategically aligned.

Without trained SEO professionals to review and contextualize outputs, automation becomes a self-reinforcing cycle of errors.

Executives must understand that machine efficiency hides judgment gaps that only humans can fill. The fewer experts retained internally, the more blind those gaps become.

Critical Skills That Protect Discoverability

Sustained visibility requires capability across four disciplines that automation cannot replace:

1. **Structured Data and Schema Management**
    Accuracy in schema markup determines how algorithms understand your products, services, and authority.

    A single error can remove entire sections of content from AI summaries or product feeds.

2. **AI-Content Review and Fact-Checking**
    Generative text tools amplify factual drift.

    Skilled reviewers ensure each claim, citation, and compliance statement aligns with verified data sources.

3. **Analytics and Performance Interpretation**
    Automated dashboards surface numbers; analysts convert them into insight.

    Knowing when to question a metric — or when a sudden ranking change signals a governance failure — requires human pattern recognition.

4. **SEO Fundamentals Across Teams**
    Product managers, designers, and developers all influence visibility signals.

    Cross-training ensures that SEO awareness permeates daily operations rather than sitting in a disconnected function.

Blind-Spot Check

If these skills exist in only one individual or agency, resilience is an illusion.

Capability Risk as a Governance Failure

Losing even one senior SEO or analyst can create a measurable revenue drop.

When key expertise resides in a single person, resignation or reassignment can disrupt visibility performance.

Executives rarely treat this as an operational risk, yet its financial impact rivals that of downtime in other systems. Governance should treat capability loss as a quantifiable exposure — tracked, mitigated, and reviewed alongside other business risks.

Building Capability Resilience

Executives can protect visibility capability through structured measures:

- **Succession Mapping** — Identify critical SEO and analytics roles with documented handover plans.
- **Cross-Training** — Ensure content, IT, and marketing teams share baseline SEO literacy.
- **Continuous Learning** — Fund education on algorithm changes, schema standards, and AI-discovery models.
- **Vendor Oversight** — Retain institutional knowledge when agencies rotate; require data and process transfer clauses in contracts.

These are not HR exercises; they are visibility continuity plans.

Without them, automation becomes an accelerant for knowledge loss.

Red Flag

If one departure can erase discoverability for a product line, capability has been treated as a convenience, not an asset.

The Executive Mandate

The C-Suite's role is not to manage SEO operations but to guarantee their durability.

That means protecting expertise from budget cycles, embedding SEO literacy into leadership programs, and ensuring visibility reporting is on par with financial and compliance data.

Many companies have a confidential HR policy that treats valued employees as assets and requires additional incentives to retain them. SEO superstars should be placed in this group.

Human resilience is the insurance policy that keeps automation productive rather than destructive.

Summary

Automation may handle execution, but visibility governance still relies on skilled human judgment.

Executives who underinvest in expertise create a brittle system that fails the moment automation drifts.

Retaining, training, and auditing human capability is not optional overhead — it is the foundation that keeps the company visible, trustworthy, and profitable.

AI AND AUTOMATION GOVERNANCE CHECKLIST

Automation can expand opportunity or amplify risk. The distinction lies in whether executives govern its use with the same rigor they apply to finance, cybersecurity, or compliance.

This checklist converts oversight into verifiable actions — the minimum standard for maintaining control over brand visibility in an automated environment.

Governance and Accountability

Assign clear accountability for AI and SEO governance — one senior leader must own oversight for how automation affects discoverability and brand integrity. - Integrate SEO into risk and audit functions alongside cyber incidents, compliance exceptions, and financial exposure.

Oversight of Automated Outputs

- **Require human review before automation affects customers.** — Any AI system that publishes under the company's name must have a documented, auditable approval workflow. –

- **Audit automation quarterly** for unintended SEO impact in content-generation, product-feed, or metadata tools.

Visibility in Executive Dashboards

- **Include discoverability metrics in board reporting** —visibility share, AI-summary mentions, and brand-query performance belong beside financial KPIs.

- **Correlate visibility equity with customer-acquisition cost (CAC)** to translate SEO health into direct financial language.

Change Control and Review

- **Require SEO sign-off for CMS, design, or structural changes.** to prevent technical debt and ranking loss.

- **Maintain version control for all automated templates** with rollback capability and version tracking.

Capability Retention and Oversight

- **Fund skill retention and cross-training** — treat training costs as insurance, not optional spend.

- **Monitor agency and vendor continuity** with contracts that guarantee data and process transfer.

Policy and Access Control

- **Implement BYOAI ("Bring Your Own AI")** rules — employees must use only approved AI systems with logged credentials.
- **Centralize tool access and permissions** for publishing, prompting, or modifying automated outputs.

Review Frequency and Reporting

- **Conduct quarterly reviews** of visibility, automation impact, and governance maturity to identify degradation or improvement.
- **Establish escalation protocols** for visibility incidents with defined notification paths and corrective actions. Automation magnifies both competence and neglect. Strong governance converts technology into performance leverage; weak governance converts it into exposure. Executives don't need to manage SEO — they need to own its continuity, measurement, and accountability.

DISASTER RECOVERY AND CONTINUITY GOVERNANCE

Why the C-Suite Must Validate Readiness

Website outages, data loss, or infrastructure breaches don't just halt transactions — they erase visibility.

A visibility outage is a brand outage: when search engines and AI assistants cannot reach verified data, your organization disappears from consideration.

Executives must treat digital continuity as an extension of visibility governance, not a separate IT concern.

Leadership Expectations and Drills

Boards already demand cybersecurity testing. The same cadence should apply to discoverability resilience:

- Annual disaster-recovery drills that simulate CMS or hosting failure.
- Verification that backups include schema, redirects, and metadata — not only content files.
- A defined Recovery Time Objective (RTO) for restoring public-facing sites and analytics.
- Joint participation of marketing, SEO, IT, and communications teams in recovery rehearsals.

- When these drills occur, executives gain confidence that brand discoverability can be restored within hours, not weeks.

Integrating Recovery into Governance Reporting

Include DR-test outcomes in quarterly visibility-governance dashboards:

- Time taken to restore indexation and structured-data accuracy.
- Verification of post-recovery ranking stability.
- Financial estimate of lost visibility during downtime.
- This converts recovery competence into a measurable governance metric, visible to the board.

Executive Assurance

A certified, tested disaster-recovery plan is not an IT document — it is a **governance asset**.

Executives who fund and review these drills demonstrate stewardship beyond compliance: they prove the organization can remain discoverable, trustworthy, and profitable even in crisis.

Next Chapter

Even the most resilient recovery plan is only as strong as the systems and funding that sustain it.

Governance does not end when the servers restart—it extends to the investment decisions that determine whether recovery becomes routine or innovation resumes.

The next chapter shifts from crisis readiness to resource stewardship, examining how technology budgets, tooling choices, and organizational structures define the maturity of your visibility governance.

For a consolidated framework of the dashboards and metrics introduced in Chapters 5–7, see Chapter 8.

Chapter 6

TECHNOLOGY AND BUDGET GOVERNANCE

Chapter 5 showed how automation and AI can damage visibility when left ungoverned.

This chapter shifts focus from the algorithms that interpret your brand to the systems and budgets that support it.

Here, technology and funding decisions become governance levers: they determine whether SEO operates as a depreciating expense or a compounding profit engine.

Executive Summary

Your technology stack and funding model decide whether you own visibility or rent it at rising prices.

In most enterprises, visibility infrastructure—CMS, analytics, and automation tools—lacks unified ownership.

When these systems are fragmented or funded episodically, organic performance becomes expensive to recover.

This chapter reframes technology and budget as the twin enablers of sustainable visibility.

It shows how to align spend, platforms, and people under a single governance model so that search performance becomes predictable, measurable, and cost-efficient.

You'll learn how to:

- Fund SEO like cybersecurity—stable, preventive, and continually audited.
- Consolidate overlapping tools without losing insight or accountability.
- Prevent silent regression during redesigns, migrations, and "brand refreshes."
- Quantify visibility as a financial asset rather than an untracked expense.
- Protect margin by converting SEO from a cost center into a profit center.

When governance integrates technology and budget discipline, visibility stops behaving like marketing luck and starts performing like managed capital—delivering compounding returns instead of recurring rescue costs.

HOW TECHNOLOGY CHOICES AFFECT VISIBILITY INFRASTRUCTURE

Every platform decision—CMS architecture, tagging framework, analytics integration, or workflow automation—either strengthens or silently erodes discoverability.

Most enterprises underestimate how fragile visibility becomes when infrastructure decisions occur without SEO or governance oversight.

Technology is not neutral; it either builds discoverability equity or leaks it.

Warning

If your website is released without an SEO sign-off, visibility risk remains unmanaged.

Visibility as a System, Not a Stack

Executives often treat the digital stack as a set of independent tools rather than a unified visibility system.

CMS performance, CDN configuration, analytics tagging, and structured data consistency all interact to influence how search engines assess authority. **When** one element fails, compounding effects appear across conversions, ranking stability, and brand trust.

The Cost of Invisible Regression

Infrastructure failures rarely announce themselves.

A small change — a template refresh, an omitted redirect, or a schema removal — can erase years of earned authority. Because regressions occur within normal operations, losses often surface only when traffic and conversions decline.

Executives mistake the symptom (a "market shift") for the cause (a preventable regression).

Mini-Case Snapshot

A global insurer updated page layouts to align with a new brand system. Structured data vanished; featured snippets stopped showing.

Organic quotes dropped 14 percent in 60 days. Initially, "market conditions" were blamed. Recovery required 9 months and an additional $720K in paid ads to fill the gap.

The expense wasn't marketing — it was the cost of missing governance.

Governance Controls for Infrastructure Integrity

Executives should require visible, auditable controls for any system that influences crawlability, indexing, or content delivery.

Minimum expectations include:

- **SEO Change Control:** Every template, navigation, or tagging change passes review by a qualified SEO owner.

- **Timely Mini-Audit:** A short SEO audit must follow **every** infrastructure release — even when SEO was consulted during planning — to verify that no regressions, indexation losses, or schema breaks occurred in production.

- **Regression Dashboards:** Real-time monitoring of ranking volatility, crawl errors, and Core Web Vitals.

- **Rollback Capability:** Versioned templates and redirects that allow rapid reversal after failure.

- **Testing Environments:** Staging systems mirrored to production for SEO QA before deployment.

- **Access Governance:** Role-based permissions limiting who can alter metadata, schema, or index directives.

These are not technical niceties — they are operational equivalents of financial controls that prevent invisible depreciation of a visibility asset.

Linking Infrastructure to Profitability

When visibility is stable, paid-media dependency declines and margins expand.

Infrastructure discipline, therefore, delivers a measurable financial impact: fewer emergency campaigns, lower acquisition costs, and sustained revenue from organic channels.

Executives should view SEO uptime the same way they view IT system uptime — each outage incurs quantifiable opportunity loss.

Tracking these losses over time makes the business case for treating visibility governance as a profit-preservation function rather than discretionary maintenance.

Summary

Technology decisions either secure or squander discoverability equity.

Without governance — including timely post-change audits — infrastructure regressions accumulate unseen until profit margins reveal the damage.

The C-Suite's mandate is straightforward: ensure every technology investment enhances visibility as deliberately as cybersecurity protects data.

FUNDING VISIBILITY WITH THE SAME DISCIPLINE AS CYBERSECURITY

Cybersecurity receives continuous funding because executives understand the cost of a breach. Visibility requires the same level of discipline because the financial risk of losing discoverability is equally real, even if it may take longer to surface.

When visibility collapses, so do conversions, authority, and brand trust. The recovery costs, often hidden in paid-media budgets, are equivalent to breach remediation in IT.

Visibility Budgets as Preventive Insurance

Cybersecurity funding isn't justified by daily crises but by the assurance that crises don't occur.

Visibility should be treated the same way: consistent, protected investment prevents volatility in search performance.

Executives should require baseline funding to maintain visibility infrastructure—structured data, technical optimization, and analytics—even during marketing slowdowns or reorganizations. Visibility maintenance is not discretionary spend; it's brand insurance.

Red Flag

If paid spend rises faster than organic growth, margin erosion is already underway. If change budgets exclude SEO verification, recovery funding will appear later under "crisis management.

From Campaign Spend to Infrastructure Spend

Traditional marketing budgets fund campaigns; governance budgets fund stability.

Treating SEO as infrastructure means allocating fixed annual resources to prevent regressions and preserve discoverability.

The model is simple:

- A portion of paid-media savings is redirected to visibility upkeep.
- Funding is tracked against organic contribution margins rather than campaign results.
- Investment continues even when campaigns pause — exactly as cybersecurity or compliance programs do.

This ensures visibility performance compounds rather than collapsing, and that it doesn't require expensive re-acquisition later.

Governance Integration with Finance

Budget governance should connect visibility metrics directly to financial indicators:

- **Visibility Equity vs. Paid CAC** — tracks the balance between earned and purchased attention.
- **Cost to Reacquire Lost Visibility** — quantifies the impact of neglect.
- **Organic Contribution Margin** — expresses SEO performance in profitability language.

When these figures appear on dashboards alongside operating income or marketing ROI, visibility gains financial parity with other managed assets.

Linking Visibility Spend to Executive Accountability

Board-level accountability must extend beyond "marketing performance" to "visibility stability."

Each fiscal year should include a governance review confirming that:

1. Visibility funding was continuous.

2. Mini-audits occurred after all system changes.

3. No regressions required for unplanned paid-media compensation.

Treating these metrics as part of the audit cycle formalizes SEO as a governed business function rather than a discretionary activity.

Summary

Both visibility governance and cybersecurity require continuous funding, documented audits, and executive accountability. Every major change to technology or content systems must include a funded SEO audit — not as a quality check, but as a governance control.

Stable budgets and routine verification convert visibility from a marketing line item into a managed, compounding business asset.

TOOLING GOVERNANCE — LESS CHAOS, MORE CLARITY

Unmanaged tooling is one of the most common causes of wasted visibility spend. Each department licenses its own SEO, analytics, or automation platform, creating redundant data, conflicting reports, and untraceable performance changes.

Without executive oversight, tool proliferation quietly converts operational spend into recurring waste — and makes accountability impossible.

The Governance Problem

Too many tools promise insight while fragmenting control.

Marketing and SEO run one analytics platform, developers use another, and agencies report through their own dashboards. Executives see dozens of metrics but no single truth.

Tooling chaos leads to duplicated effort, conflicting interpretations, and undetected regressions when multiple systems rewrite or automate metadata.

Governance Check

If a vendor salesperson can describe your visibility performance better than your internal dashboards, then your tooling is driving strategy rather than supporting it.

Consolidation and Standardization

Executives should treat the digital toolset as the financial system of record—singular, auditable, and standardized.

Mandate:

- One Analytics Source of Truth: All departments reference the same analytics and attribution system.
- Unified Crawling and Monitoring Tools: Use standardized site crawlers and visibility trackers across markets and agencies.
- Central Data Repository: Store keyword, schema, and content metrics in one governed platform for version control and trend analysis.
- Role-Based Access: Restrict modification privileges; assign read-only access broadly but editing rights narrowly.

Tool consolidation is not just about cost reduction; it is about restoring control.

One dashboard means one narrative, enabling executives to tie visibility metrics directly to financial outcomes.

Governance Funding and Mini-Audit Cadence

These audits should verify:

- Data synchronization across analytics, CRM, and content systems
- Proper tagging and event tracking after CMS or UX updates
- Security and privacy compliance for all data-sharing integrations

When audits are funded and scheduled as routine governance tasks, tooling accuracy becomes predictable instead of incidental.

Tool ROI and Renewal Discipline

Each tool must either **improve discoverability** or **reduce risk** — otherwise, sunset it.

Before renewal, require a simple ROI justification:

- What measurable visibility gain did this tool enable?
- What process or compliance risk did it mitigate?
- Can its output be replicated by an existing system?

Executives should expect annual reports showing tool overlap, utilization rates, and renewal recommendations. Treat each renewal as a board-level purchasing decision; every license line is an implicit statement of visibility governance.

Note: Many enterprise-grade tools are expensive and often tied to a specific user on a specific computer. If they don't use it sufficiently, ask them to justify a renewal.

Metrics for Tooling Effectiveness

Governance maturity can be tracked through a few simple indicators:

1. **Tool Redundancy Ratio:** Number of overlapping licenses vs. active users.

2. **Audit Pass Rate:** Percentage of quarterly mini-audits completed without regression.

3. **Data Consistency Index:** Variance between different analytics or rank-tracking systems.

4. **Visibility Correlation:** Degree to which consolidated dashboards align with financial KPIs.

Executives can review these quarterly reports during audit or risk committee meetings.

Consistency across tools proves visibility is governed; variance signals fragmentation.

Summary

Tooling is the nervous system of visibility governance.

Without consolidation, oversight, and audit funding, tools multiply faster than accountability.

Executives who centralize control, enforce mini-audit cadence, and demand ROI transparency convert tooling spend from chaotic cost to measurable performance infrastructure.

Technology Choices as AI Visibility Decisions

Technology governance now directly influences whether your organization is eligible for AI-mediated discovery. Infrastructure decisions that once affected only performance or reliability now shape how search engines and AI systems interpret, summarize, and recommend your brand.

Executives should understand that AI visibility is not created by tools alone—but they can quietly constrain it.

Common technology decisions with unintended AI visibility consequences include:

- CMS platforms that fragment structured data across templates
- Headless or JavaScript-heavy architectures that obscure core content from crawlers
- Over-aggressive caching or CDN rules that delay content updates reaching AI systems
- Third-party plugins that inject duplicate or conflicting metadata
- Security layers that block or throttle legitimate AI crawlers without policy intent

None of these issues appear as line items in an SEO budget. It's more likely that SEO isn't consulted before Engineering begins considering such platform changes. They surface later as reduced inclusion, misrepresentation, or reliance on paid channels to compensate.

Mature organizations treat technology selection as a visibility decision. They require teams to answer not just:

"Does this tool improve efficiency?"

but also:

"How does this affect machine interpretation of our content?"

This framing changes budget conversations. Investments in clean markup, accessible rendering, stable URLs, and structured feeds are no longer discretionary optimizations—they are eligibility controls.

Executives who govern technology with AI visibility in mind fund fewer tools, demand clearer standards, and avoid costly remediation after discovery pathways have already shifted.

Technology governance is no longer just about stack hygiene. It is about protecting the organization's right to be understood by systems that increasingly decide who gets seen.

CHANGE-CONTROL GOVERNANCE — TECHNICAL PROCESS AND PROTOCOLS

While Chapter 4 addressed organizational continuity during change, this section focuses on the technical disciplines and process controls that prevent regression in visibility during platform migrations, redesigns, and system updates.

Most visibility losses occur not in crisis, but during normal operations — a redesign, a CMS upgrade, or a product migration executed without structured oversight.

Executives rarely see the damage until months later, when organic performance slides and paid budgets silently expand to compensate.

Change-control governance is the discipline that prevents this erosion by treating every system modification as a potential financial event.

Where Regressions Hide

High-risk scenarios are predictable and repeatable:

1. **Platform Migrations**

   - Budgets flow to new templates, integrations, and rebranding while redirects, legacy URLs, or structured data are trimmed to meet deadlines.

   - The new platform launches "on time" — and organic traffic collapses for six months.

2. **Design Refreshes**

    - Navigation structures change, internal links shrink, and content hierarchies shift without authority mapping.

    - Algorithms interpret these changes as a loss of relevance rather than an improvement in design.

3. **CMS or Automation Enhancements**

    - Tagging systems are rewritten, metadata fields are deprecated, or QA steps are bypassed.

    - Crawlability weakens and critical pages drop from indexation without immediate warning.

Blind-Spot Check

If no one can clearly explain how a change affects Google's or AI platforms' ability to understand your content, stop the release.

Governance Requirements Before and After Change

Executives should enforce a dual-phase governance protocol for any change that touches visibility infrastructure:

- **Pre-Change Approval**

  - All navigation, template, or metadata adjustments must receive SEO sign-off confirming that redirects, structured data, and internal link equity are preserved.

- **Post-Change Mini-Audit**

  - Within 48–72 hours of deployment, commission a short SEO audit — regardless of prior consultation — to validate live production results.

  - The audit confirms indexing health, schema accuracy, Core Web Vitals, and link continuity.

- o Funding for this step must be built into every project's lifecycle budget.

- o Post-change audits are the visibility equivalent of a financial reconciliation: they catch what planning missed.

Regression Dashboards and Rollback Protocols

Governance should mandate the following controls:

- **Regression Dashboards:** Real-time tracking of ranking volatility, crawl errors, and site-speed deviations.

- **Rollback Capability:** Version control and backup redirects allow for the fast reversal of failed deployments.

- **Change Ledger:** Document every release affecting visibility — what changed, who approved it, and what the measured impact was.

- **Alert Thresholds:** Define quantitative triggers (e.g., 10% traffic drop or sudden schema error surge) that automatically escalate to executives.

These measures turn visibility protection from reactive troubleshooting into proactive risk management.

Linking Change Governance to Financial Performance

Visibility regression has a measurable cost.

Each technical failure increases paid-media dependence, raises acquisition costs, and depresses organic conversion rates.

Executives should request quarterly reporting that translates visibility incidents into financial terms—the cost to reacquire traffic lost due to unmanaged change.

This turns change-control governance into a budget-protection mechanism rather than an operational checklist.

Summary

Every system release is a potential visibility event.

Without structured governance, minor updates quietly compound into multi-million-dollar recovery projects.

Pre-approval, funded post-change audits, and rollback protocols convert change management from a technical procedure into a measurable safeguard of profitability.

BUDGETING FOR CAPABILITY AND RESILIENCE

Technology protects systems. People protect visibility.

No amount of automation or infrastructure spend can compensate for the loss of institutional SEO expertise.

Executives often approve capital budgets for new platforms but overlook the smaller, ongoing investment that sustains the human capability required to govern them.

This omission converts skill attrition into silent revenue loss.

Warning

If headcount decisions ignore the impact on visibility, you are risking revenue unthinkingly.

The Governance Case for Capability Funding

SEO capability is not a discretionary skill set; it is operational insurance.

Governance frameworks fail without people who understand both how algorithms evaluate content and how systems transmit that content to search and AI platforms.

Executives should treat visibility expertise as a controlled competency — tracked, maintained, and audited just like cybersecurity credentials or financial certifications.

Losing one key specialist can trigger a cascade of visibility failures that no software can automatically repair.

Integrating Capability Funding into Financial Governance

Capability funding should appear as a defined line item within visibility budgets — not hidden under "training" or "marketing overhead."

Executives should review it annually alongside infrastructure spend and automation licensing.

Performance indicators may include:

1. Number of certified visibility professionals retained or trained each year
2. Cross-departmental SEO awareness sessions completed
3. Time to restore visibility after staff turnover or vendor transition

These metrics directly link human capability to risk management and margin protection.

The Audit Connection

Every major infrastructure or automation change should trigger a **post-change mini-SEO audit, which requires skilled personnel** to execute.

Budgeting for these recurring reviews ensures they occur reliably rather than being skipped when resources tighten.

Executives should verify that audit capacity — internal or external — exists year-round, not only during crises.

Capability funding ensures that governance controls can be implemented.

Framing Capability as a Financial Asset

Treat expertise as a renewable asset that compounds value over time.

When teams retain and expand their visibility knowledge, they shorten recovery cycles, improve ROI from existing tools, and prevent costly regressions.

The financial model is straightforward: **invest in expertise → reduce incident frequency → protect profit margins.**

Financial Warning

If cost savings from staff reductions exceed the next quarter's training budget, the risk of visibility is rising faster than capability maturity.

Summary

Sustained visibility requires sustained human expertise.

Executives who underfund capability create brittle systems that fail when personnel change or automation drifts.

Budgeting for skill retention, training, and post-change audits transforms SEO resilience from individual brilliance into institutional governance.

The return is measurable: shorter recovery times, lower acquisition costs, and greater operational continuity.

Technology and budget governance require visibility metrics that connect organic performance to financial impact. Chapter 8 details the executive dashboard framework, including the Financial Visibility Dashboard owned by the CFO, which translates search performance into margin protection and cost-efficiency indicators.

TECHNOLOGY AND BUDGET GOVERNANCE CHECKLIST

Governance turns visibility from a marketing dependency into a managed financial asset.

This checklist translates the chapter's principles into a repeatable oversight routine for the C-Suite.

Quarterly Governance Actions

Use this checklist as part of your board or executive review process:

- ☐ **Technology decisions include visibility risk evaluation.**
  Every major platform, CMS, or design investment must include SEO and discoverability impact analysis.

- ☐ **Visibility infrastructure receives stable funding.**
  Annual budgets must include maintenance allocations, not just campaign spend.

- ☐ **Tooling is consolidated under governance.**
  All analytics, crawling, and reporting tools must be rolled into a single, governed source of truth.

- ☐ **No system changes bypass SEO review.**
  All deployments that affect navigation, templates, metadata, or structured data require sign-off from a qualified SEO stakeholder.

- ☐ **Post-change mini-audits are mandatory.**
  A short SEO audit must follow every infrastructure change — regardless of prior consultation — to verify indexing, schema, and link integrity.

- ☐ **Regression dashboards and rollback plans exist.**
  Monitoring and version control systems must be ready before launch, not after failure.

☐ **Budgets protect capability as much as technology.**
Training, cross-functional literacy, and succession planning are funded annually.

☐ **Visibility metrics appear on financial dashboards.**
Track organic share, paid CAC trends, and reacquisition costs alongside standard performance indicators.

☐ **Audit cadence is funded and predictable.**
Quarterly visibility audits are scheduled and budgeted, not discretionary.

☐ **Visibility equity is reviewed like infrastructure health.**
Treat organic visibility as a renewable asset with measurable maturity stages.

Executive Insight

You don't control algorithms or platforms, but you do control the systems, budgets, and skills that influence how your business is represented and discovered. Technology either compounds your visibility equity or mortgages it. Strong governance ensures every dollar spent builds durable discoverability and measurable return.

Chapter Transition: From Oversight to Measurement

Governance defines accountability, but measurement proves its value. The next chapter shows how executives can interpret visibility data as a true performance system rather than a marketing signal.

Chapter 7

MEASURING WHAT MATTERS — PERFORMANCE, RISK, AND OPPORTUNITY

EXECUTIVE SUMMARY

You cannot manage what you do not see — and most organizations still cannot see the true value or vulnerability of their organic visibility.

This chapter shows you how to measure search performance as a revenue protection measure, not as vanity metrics. You'll learn how to evaluate:

- Your visibility equity — the digital real estate you own vs. rent
- Competitive exposure — where rivals can steal demand before you notice
- Revenue sensitivity — how much profit depends on discoverability
- Alignment with future discovery models — including multimodal and AI-led search

When you measure visibility strategically, SEO shifts from a cost line to a resilience indicator with board-level accountability.

WHY EXECUTIVE MEASUREMENT MUST CHANGE

The Visibility Gap You Don't See

Most dashboards show what you receive, not what you miss.

Executives need a clear view of:

- The market demand you are eligible to win
- The share you currently earn
- The revenue left on the table each quarter

Marketing often reports traffic growth while competitors quietly absorb profitable demand.

Red Flag

If the only organic metric you see is "traffic," you are governing an outcome — not a strategy.

Performance as Revenue Protection

Visibility failure rarely announces itself. It begins with:

- Slow regression in high-intent rankings
- Rising cost of paid acquisition
- Less trustworthy representation in conversational and AI-generated results

These effects may take quarters to show up in revenue, but costs increase immediately.

Your metrics must reveal decline before customers do.

Volatility and Inconsistency in AI-Mediated Visibility

Traditional search engines normalize enormous volumes of similar queries behind the scenes. Non-personalized searches are clustered, standardized, and resolved against a stable index, which is why two executives typing broadly similar queries are likely to see materially identical results pages. This makes rank-based reporting feel dependable, even if it masks complexity.

Large language models operate very differently. They do not retrieve results from a fixed index in response to a query; they generate responses probabilistically, synthesizing language based on learned patterns rather than selecting from a ranked list. As a result, identical prompts can produce different brand mentions, different ordering, or different omissions from one response to the next. This variability is not evidence that visibility is unstable; it is evidence that the measurement paradigm has changed. Snapshot metrics and single-response checks are structurally unreliable indicators of AI-mediated presence.

Executive visibility governance, therefore, requires **verification through repetition, pattern analysis, and trend observation over time**—measuring how frequently and consistently the organization is referenced across prompts, contexts, and categories, rather than where it appears in any one response. Without this distinction, leadership teams risk interpreting normal probabilistic behavior as volatility and reacting to noise rather than governing signal integrity.

Executive takeaway: AI-mediated visibility must be monitored as a pattern over time, not as a position at a point in time, which is why executive dashboards must evolve from rank reporting to governance-grade indicators of presence, consistency, and risk.

FROM REPORTING TO MANAGEMENT — A SHIFT IN PURPOSE

Most organizations *report* SEO results, but few actually *manage* them.

Reports describe outcomes; governance explains causes and prescribes action.

Executives need visibility data that answers three questions:

1. **Performance** — Is visibility improving relative to investment?

2. **Risk** — Where could we lose it?

3. **Opportunity** — Where can we expand it most efficiently?
   Traditional dashboards satisfy curiosity; governance dashboards support decisions.
   This distinction turns measurement into management.

The Measurement Blind Spot — Influence Without Clicks

Traditional SEO measurement assumes a visible chain of events: a query, a click, on-site engagement, and a measurable outcome. That assumption no longer holds consistently. AI-mediated search systems increasingly summarize, compare, and recommend without sending users to a website, yet those interactions still shape decisions.

This creates a structural measurement blind spot. Analytics platforms capture what happens after a click, but they cannot observe when an AI system has already influenced perception, preference, or choice upstream. As a result, organizations may see declining organic traffic alongside stable revenue, rising branded demand, or improved conversion efficiency in other channels. Without context, this divergence is often misread as SEO underperformance rather than a shift in how visibility operates.

For executives, this is not a tooling problem but a governance one. Measurement frameworks built solely around deterministic events—sessions, clicks, and attributed conversions—fail to capture influence outside the website. Visibility in AI-led discovery environments is probabilistic, not positional. Each interaction is a fresh evaluation in which your brand may or may not appear, regardless of prior performance.

This means that the absence of a click does not equal the absence of impact. Influence may occur without attribution, and demand may be shaped before traditional metrics activate. Executive measurement must therefore expand beyond traffic outcomes to include consistency of presence, accuracy of representation, and comparative inclusion across machine-mediated discovery surfaces.

The next section reframes measurement around performance, risk, and opportunity—dimensions that remain valid even when influence becomes indirect, distributed, and partially invisible.

INDEPENDENT VERIFICATION OF AI-MEDIATED VISIBILITY

Some forms of digital visibility cannot be observed solely through dashboards. One supplementary source of evidence is standard website access records—often referred to as website logs. These records capture every site visit, whether from a human browser or an automated data-collection system.

Increasingly, those automated visitors include AI systems that read, summarize, and reuse website content to generate answers elsewhere. While these records do not show intent or outcomes, they confirm that machine systems are accessing specific pages at specific times and at a measurable scale. For executives, this serves as an assurance signal: independent evidence that the organization's content is being read and processed by both people and machines, even when no clicks, visits, or conversions appear in analytics reports.

THE THREE DIMENSIONS OF VISIBILITY OVERSIGHT

Executives need one view across performance, risk, and opportunity.

Performance — Owned Visibility Equity

Track quarterly:

- Share of impressions for high-value search terms
- Page-level performance along critical journeys
- Visibility equity vs. paid CAC trends
- Return on incremental organic investment

This shows how much free revenue you retain — or lose — each quarter.

Ask your team:

"How much would EBITDA drop if our organic visibility fell 20% next quarter?"

If no one knows, you are already exposed.

Risk — Structural Fragility and Regression Signals

Visibility loss is often preventable — if risk indicators exist:

- Page experience or Core Web Vitals decline
- Indexation drops after deployments or migrations
- Increased reliance on paid channels to hold steady
- Talent gaps or specialized turnover
- AI summaries or recommendation engines misrepresenting your brand

Red Flag

Paid growth masking declining organic share = silent margin leak.

AI Visibility Risk Is Systemic, Not Volatile

Traditional SEO risk behaves like market volatility. Rankings fluctuate, competitors advance, algorithms update—and recovery is usually possible with time and investment.

AI-mediated visibility introduces a different category of risk: systemic exclusion.

When AI systems stop selecting your organization as a reference source, the impact is not gradual. Your brand may disappear entirely from synthesized answers, recommendations, and briefings—while traditional dashboards remain deceptively calm.

From an executive standpoint, this matters because:

- AI summaries do not degrade linearly; they switch sources
- Once a competitor becomes the "default explanation," displacement is difficult
- Visibility loss may occur without traffic loss, masking exposure
- Recovery depends on structural clarity, not tactical optimization

This creates a governance problem, not a marketing problem.

Executives should treat AI visibility risk similarly to credit risk or supplier concentration risk: low frequency, high impact, and poorly detected by standard reporting.

Early indicators of systemic AI exclusion include:

- Competitors are consistently named in AI summaries, while you are omitted
- Your brand appearing only in historical or generic contexts
- AI assistants mischaracterizing your offerings or positioning
- Citations shifting toward aggregators, marketplaces, or secondary sources

None of these appear reliably in analytics tools. They require deliberate executive inquiry and periodic inspection.

This is why AI visibility must be reviewed as part of risk governance, not delegated solely to performance teams. If leadership does not ask how AI systems describe the organization, no dashboard will surface the answer.

The executive mandate is simple: ensure your organization remains explainable, referenceable, and selectable when machines—not people—mediate discovery.

Opportunity — Competitive Takeover Watch

Your demand pipeline is visible in the search results.

Track:

- Top 100–200 category drivers
- Share vs. leaders and disruptors
- Structured data coverage for emerging result types
- Trends where a rival gains an early advantage

This becomes a future revenue radar.

Example

A bank lost 32% query share for business loan refinancing in two quarters — without a revenue warning — because a competitor added relevant schema markup and expert content.

FUTURE-PROOFING DISCOVERABILITY

Preparing For AI-Led Discovery

Search is shifting from lists of links to:

- Summaries
- Answers
- Turning-point recommendations
- Multimodal recognition

Measurement must include:

- Share of citations within AI summaries
- Product accuracy and prominence in recommendations
- Entity strength for brand, products, and experts
- Voice and image search relevance

Executive Expectation

AI visibility is probabilistic, not fixed. Each conversation is a new timeline where your brand may appear, fade, or vanish depending on prior context and platform resets.

Leaders should measure citation consistency across timelines, not just frequency. Success is not about "ranking higher" but about maximizing the probability of consistent brand presence in answers.

Executive Question

"How are AI assistants currently describing us — and is it accurate?"

Visibility Beyond the Website

Your influence extends to:

- Retailer and marketplace listings
- Support and knowledge ecosystems
- Structured data and feeds across platforms

You own little of this — but you shape all of it.

Measurement Must Anticipate Loss, Not Just Explain Performance

Most executive dashboards explain what already happened. That is insufficient for governing visibility in machine-mediated discovery environments.

Search visibility rarely collapses suddenly. **It decays.** By the time revenue declines, the underlying loss of discoverability has already occurred—often quarters earlier. AI-mediated systems accelerate this pattern by reallocating attention invisibly, without clicks, impressions, or obvious warning signals.

This creates a leadership obligation: **measurement must surface** *exposure* **before it becomes an** *outcome.*

Executives should expect visibility reporting to answer not only "How are we performing?" but also:

- Where would visibility loss hurt us most?
- Which revenue streams are structurally dependent on discoverability?
- How quickly could AI-mediated summaries redirect demand away from us?
- Which changes would reduce our probability of being selected as the answer?

This shifts measurement from descriptive analytics to anticipatory governance. Metrics should highlight sensitivity, concentration, and fragility—not just growth or decline.

A practical way to operationalize this is through scenario-based visibility exposure. Instead of forecasting traffic, leadership reviews modeled questions such as:

"If AI-mediated discovery reduced our presence in this category by 20 percent, what margin impact would follow—and how quickly?"

These scenarios transform SEO measurement into a risk discipline comparable to supply-chain, cybersecurity, or regulatory exposure analysis.

When measurement anticipates loss, executives gain time. Time to intervene, reallocate resources, or correct signal drift before markets notice. When it only explains performance, leadership is already reacting too late.

BOARD-READY VISIBILITY REPORTING

Executives require one slide per quarter showing:

- Organic share of revenue vs. paid CAC

- Branded and non-branded visibility trends
- Top opportunity to capture
- Top structural risk to mitigate
- Exposure scenarios by revenue impact

When visibility equity appears next to margin and risk, decisions shift.

Warning

If SEO performance appears only in marketing reviews, it will never shape strategy.

EXECUTIVE QUESTIONS THAT DRIVE ACCOUNTABILITY

- Are we gaining or losing non-branded market share?
- How much revenue is at risk from search volatility?
- What demand signals show future growth opportunities?
- Are AI-generated summaries accurate and favorably positioned?
- Which competitor threatens our discoverability the most?

Every question signals priority and changes behavior.

EXECUTIVE INSIGHT

Your competitors do not need to outperform you everywhere — only where customers search and algorithms decide.

Measure visibility like a strategic asset — and you will protect margin, anticipate threats, and accelerate into new demand before others see it.

LEADERSHIP REMINDER

You can **outsource tasks**, but you cannot outsource **accountability** for visibility.

Governance maturity isn't perfection. It's prevention.

The next chapter has a consolidated framework of the dashboards and metrics introduced in Chapters 5–7.

Chapter 8

PURPOSE

Dashboards are the board's window into visibility performance. They translate governance outcomes into measurable, repeatable signals. This section consolidates all dashboard requirements discussed throughout the book, so leaders can confidently delegate construction.

In this book, dashboards are not standalone measurement systems. They are **presentation layers for the Visibility Governance Maturity Model (VGMM)** and its contributing domain models, designed to make governance outcomes visible to executives. The dashboards described here summarize maturity signals, audit results, and risk indicators already produced through governed processes, rather than introducing new scoring frameworks or parallel assessments.

TWO DASHBOARD CATEGORIES: MATURITY AND PERFORMANCE

Executives need visibility into two fundamentally different questions:

- "Are we performing well?"
- "Can we sustain that performance?"

These questions require **different** measurement systems.

Operational Performance Dashboards measure business outcomes:

- traffic trends
- ranking positions

- conversion rates
- AI citation frequency, and
- revenue attribution.

These dashboards draw from analytics platforms, Search Console, and AI monitoring tools. **They answer whether visibility is working today.**

Governance Maturity Dashboards measure process health:

- whether single points of failure (SPOFs) have been identified and addressed,
- whether ownership is documented and active,
- whether training is current,
- whether audits occur on schedule, and
- whether escalation procedures exist and function.

These dashboards draw from governance tracking systems, process documentation, and capability assessments. **They answer whether visibility will remain reliable tomorrow.**

The distinction matters because performance and governance do not move in lockstep. An organization can achieve strong visibility performance temporarily through individual heroics. At the same time, governance remains weak—creating fragility that compounds invisibly until a key person departs or a system change breaks what was never structurally protected. Conversely, investing in governance maturity may not yield immediate performance gains, but it builds a foundation for sustained, scalable results that endure transitions.

Boards that confuse the two often make one of two errors: funding governance improvements while demanding immediate performance returns, or celebrating performance improvements without questioning whether they depend on unsustainable conditions. Both errors expose the organization to preventable risk.

Operational dashboards show *if* you are succeeding. Governance dashboards show *whether* that success is sustainable.

The five dashboards described in this chapter include both types. The **Capability and Maturity Dashboard** specifically tracks governance maturity—whether your processes, people, and structures are positioned to protect visibility regardless of personnel changes, platform shifts, or market disruptions. The remaining four dashboards track operational performance, though each incorporates governance inputs to contextualize whether trends reflect structural strength or temporary conditions.

When both dashboard types are reviewed together, executives gain the complete picture: current performance plus the organizational readiness required to sustain it.

VISIBILITY PERFORMANCE DASHBOARD (Operational)
Q4 2025

Organic Traffic:	847K visits	↑ +12%
Ranking Positions:	Top 3: 43%	↑ +5%
AI Citations:	892 mentions	↑ +18%
Conversion Rate:	3.2%	→ stable
Organic Revenue:	$2.4M	↑ +9%

Figure 4 Visibility Performance Dashboard: Measuring Business Outcomes and Market Results

VGMM Governance Maturity Dashboard
Q4 2025 • Executive Review

OVERALL MATURITY SCORE: 3.2 / 5.0 (SPOF-capped at 2)
Status: STRUCTURED (Developing processes)
Trend: ↑ +0.3 vs. Q3

DOMAIN MATURITY SCORES:
Content Governance   3.5 / 5.0 ●●●○○
* SPOFs: 1 identified (schema lead)
* Ownership: Documented

SEO Governance   3.0 / 5.0 ●●●○○
* SPOFs: 2 identified (tech SEO, analytics)
* Training: 85% complete

Website Performance Gov.   3.8 / 5.0 ●●●●○
* Escalation path: Active
* Change control: Enforced

Accessibility Governance   2.5 / 5.0 ●●○○○
* SPOFs: 3 identified ⚠
* Audit: Overdue 45 days

Workflow & Execution Gov.   2.8 / 5.0 ●●○○○
* Process documentation: Incomplete
* Cross-training: In progress

CRITICAL GOVERNANCE GAPS
* 6 total SPOFs identified across domains
* Accessibility audit overdue (remediation plan)
* Workflow documentation incomplete (Q1 target)

Figure 5 VGMM Governance Maturity Dashboard: Measuring Process Health and Organizational Readiness

CORE DASHBOARDS AND THEIR PURPOSE

Dashboard	Primary Owner	Decision Supported
Visibility Governance Dashboard	CVO	Overall organic share, risk, and recovery costs
Financial Visibility Dashboard	CFO / Finance	Margin protection, cost to reacquire visibility, paid vs. organic ROI
Change-Control Dashboard	CTO / Product	Regression tracking after deployments or migrations
Capability and Maturity Dashboard	HR / Governance Office	Skill retention, training cadence, and maturity signals derived from VGMM capability assessments
AI & Automation Impact Dashboard	Chief Digital Officer	Brand accuracy and visibility in AI-generated results

KEY METRICS TO INCLUDE

These are examples. In practice, each business may have a slightly different set of VGMM metrics to monitor.

Visibility Performance

- Organic share of total search revenue
- Visibility equity vs. paid CAC trend
- Cost to reacquire lost visibility
- Forecast investment for infrastructure health

Risk and Regression

- Indexation rate after deployments
- Core Web Vitals trend
- Traffic volatility by content type
- Number of failed audits or unmitigated regressions

Capability and Compliance

- SEO training hours and certifications retained
- Cross-functional literacy coverage (Product, Legal, Comms)
- Audit cadence adherence

AI and Emerging Discovery

- Share of citations in AI summaries
- Brand and product accuracy score in AI outputs
- Structured data coverage for new result types

REPORTING CADENCE

- **Monthly** — Operational dashboards for SEO and IT managers.

- **Quarterly** — Executive roll-up including financial and governance metrics.

- **Annually** — Board summary comparing visibility equity vs. infrastructure maturity.

Each dashboard should integrate directly into existing BI or financial-reporting tools (e.g., Power BI, Tableau, Looker) to avoid "SEO-only" silos.

INTEGRATING REVIEW CYCLES ACROSS GOVERNANCE FUNCTIONS

The quarterly and annual reviews described throughout this book are not independent activities. They consolidate into the unified dashboard cadences outlined above.

How functional reviews feed the dashboard system:

- **Chapter 4's governance compliance reporting** (publishing standards, technical health, regression tracking) flows into the monthly operational dashboards and quarterly executive roll-ups.
- **Chapter 5's automation impact and capability assessments** (AI content oversight, skill retention, automation risks) feed the Capability and Maturity Dashboard and AI & Automation Impact Dashboard.
- **Chapter 6's technology and budget reviews** (tool consolidation, change control, infrastructure decisions) populate the Financial Visibility Dashboard and Change-Control Dashboard.
- **Chapter 7's measurement frameworks** (performance, risk, and opportunity metrics) provide the foundational data for the Visibility Governance Dashboard.

Organizations should not create separate quarterly review meetings for each governance domain. That approach generates meeting fatigue, dilutes executive attention, and fragments accountability. Instead, each functional area contributes its metrics to the unified dashboard system described in this chapter. The dashboards consolidate all governance signals—compliance, automation, technology, financial, and performance—into integrated views that executives and boards review at established quarterly and annual cadences.

The result: One quarterly executive review, not five. One annual board summary, not multiple disconnected reports. All governance dimensions are visible simultaneously, enabling pattern recognition and integrated decision-making that siloed reviews cannot deliver.

When visibility governance integrates with existing corporate reporting cycles—quarterly business reviews, audit committee meetings, board strategy sessions—it gains legitimacy and durability. Executives do not need new meetings to govern visibility. They need visibility metrics incorporated into the meetings that already determine resource allocation, risk mitigation, and strategic priorities.

This consolidation prevents the organizational anti-pattern in which each governance initiative requires its own review cadence, creating calendar congestion that ultimately undermines all governance efforts. Visibility governance succeeds when it becomes part of how the organization already operates, not an addition that competes for attention.

DELEGATION FRAMEWORK

When the CEO or board requests visibility of governance dashboards:

1. Assign executive ownership per dashboard.

2. Allocate development budget from visibility governance funding.

3. Mandate that post-change mini-audit results flow automatically into these dashboards.

4. Require quarterly visibility summaries in board packs.

IMPLEMENTATION SEQUENCE — TURNING DASHBOARDS INTO ACTION

Dashboards turn governance into visibility you can manage.

To ensure they function as decision systems—not just reports—follow this implementation sequence.

Each step connects ownership, accountability, and funding so the dashboards remain reliable and meaningful over time.

Step 1 — Assign Ownership

Visibility governance crosses multiple departments.

Assign one accountable executive for each dashboard category:

- **Financial and Visibility Dashboard** → CFO or VP of Finance

- **Change-Control Dashboard** → CTO or Head of Product

- **Capability and Maturity Dashboard** → CHRO or Head of Governance

- **AI and Automation Dashboard** → Chief Digital Officer or Innovation Lead

- **Overall Visibility Governance Dashboard** → CMO or SEO Program Director

Ownership ensures data is interpreted within the right context and reported consistently.

Step 2 — Consolidate Data Sources

Data scattered across tools undermines credibility.

Integrate all metrics—search, analytics, CRM, and financial—into a single BI platform such as Power BI, Tableau, or Looker.

Require all vendors and internal teams to provide standardized exports that support these dashboards.

Governance must designate a single "source of truth" for each metric to prevent version conflicts.

Step 3 — Define Reporting Cadence

Set a routine that aligns visibility with other governance cycles:

Cadence	Audience	Purpose
Monthly	SEO & Operations Teams	Monitor regressions and quick wins
Quarterly	Executives & Board Committees	Evaluate visibility performance, risk, and opportunity
Annually	Board of Directors	Review long-term visibility equity vs. financial outcomes

Cadence prevents dashboard drift and turns data review into a leadership habit.

Step 4 — Link Mini-Audits to Dashboards

Every infrastructure or content change should automatically trigger a post-change, mini-SEO audit.

Audit results—such as regression status, schema integrity, and indexing checks—should flow directly into the dashboard's quarterly summaries.

This creates a feedback loop: governance detects issues, dashboards visualize them, and funding decisions follow evidence.

Step 5 — Embed Accountability and Incentives

Dashboards only matter if behavior changes.

Integrate visibility metrics into:

- **Departmental OKRs** (e.g., "Reduce cost-to-reacquire visibility by 20%").

- **Performance Reviews** for senior managers who influence content, design, or technology.

- **Vendor Contracts**, requiring agencies to maintain or improve dashboard KPIs.

When metrics are tied to incentives, visibility governance becomes self-sustaining.

Step 6 — Audit, Update, and Evolve

Dashboards mature as your data and governance evolve.

Schedule an annual "dashboard audit" to verify data accuracy, metric relevance, and automation reliability.

Add or retire metrics as AI search behavior changes, but preserve historical comparability so trends remain meaningful.

A dashboard that cannot explain change is decoration, not governance.

Executive Insight

A dashboard is only as valuable as the decision it enables.

Treat each one as a living governance system—reviewed, updated, and funded like any other enterprise control.

When every metric has an owner, cadence, and consequence, visibility becomes measurable capital.

That's when SEO finally earns its place on the balance sheet.

Chapter 9

EXECUTIVE CHECKLIST AND SCORECARD

EXECUTIVE SUMMARY

Strong governance only succeeds when it is measurable and visible to leadership.

This chapter provides a framework for assessing your digital visibility, governance maturity, and cross-functional accountability over time. It converts principles into a quarterly scorecard — ensuring visibility remains a managed, auditable asset. It also reinforces why your senior SEO executive should be included in executive-level reporting, so strategic oversight reflects operational reality.

The scorecard in this chapter is a **governance summary**, not an independent evaluation method. It consolidates outcomes from VGMM-aligned reviews into an executive-readable format, translating maturity, audit discipline, and risk exposure into questions suitable for board and leadership discussion.

FROM DASHBOARDS TO SCORECARDS: MATURITY OVER ACTIVITY

Avoiding Label-Driven Oversight

As AI-mediated discovery has evolved, a range of new labels has emerged to describe optimization strategies, including "Answer Engine Optimization" (AEO) and "Generative Engine Optimization"

(GEO). These labels describe tactical emphases, not new governance domains.

From an executive perspective, the distinction is not operationally meaningful. What matters is whether the organization's content, systems, and workflows are governed well enough to remain eligible for retrieval, interpretation, and reuse by external decision systems. Governance should focus on readiness and risk, not on adopting or managing emerging acronyms.

Executives add the most value by overseeing overall visibility maturity and delegating domain execution to functional leaders when leadership attention shifts from exposure to labels and governance clarity erodes.

Executive oversight of search visibility succeeds only when governance boundaries are clear. The C-suite should govern **visibility maturity**, not the mechanics of how individual teams deliver it.

The Visibility Governance Maturity Model (VGMM) is the appropriate level of executive oversight. It provides leadership with a consolidated view of whether the organization's internal discipline is sufficient to protect discoverability, credibility, and margin as digital and AI-mediated environments evolve. VGMM exists to enable executives to evaluate exposure and readiness without descending into functional detail.

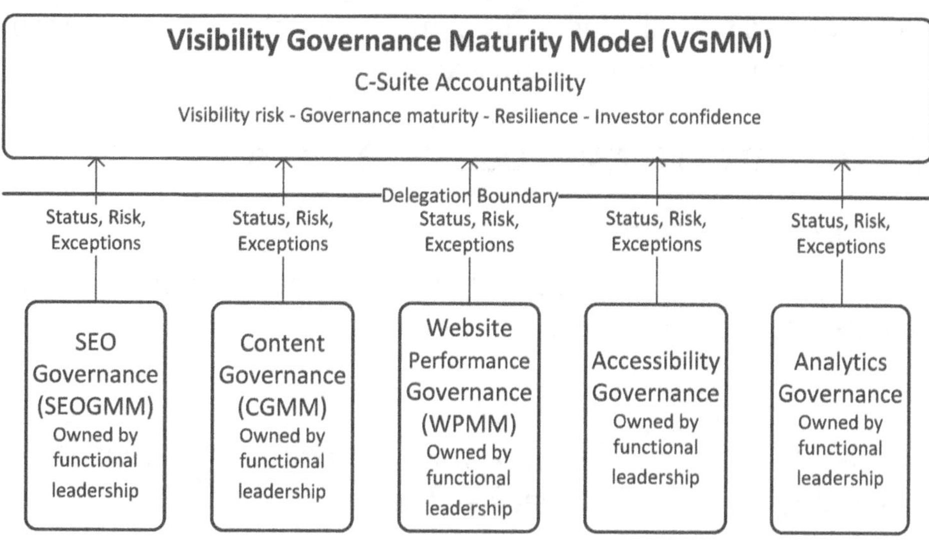

Figure 6 What the C-Suite Governs — and What It Delegates

Domain-level governance models—SEO Governance, Content Governance, Website Performance Governance, Accessibility Governance, and Analytics Governance—are management instruments. They belong with the leaders accountable for execution, remediation, and continuous improvement. When executives review domain-level maturity scores directly, governance has already failed. The signal becomes distorted, accountability blurs, and operational detail crowds out strategic judgment.

This separation is a deliberate delegation. Executives govern outcomes, risk, and investment confidence. Management governs standards, workflows, and corrective action. Information flows upward through structured reporting, exception escalation, and material risk indicators—not through raw domain scores.

Boards that respect this boundary gain clearer insight with less friction. They assess whether visibility is well-governed enough to be trusted, while teams retain the authority to fix what is broken. Mature organizations do not ask leaders to manage complexity; they design systems that make complexity governable.

USING THE CHECKLIST AS A LEADERSHIP TOOL

Why a Scorecard Matters

As an executive, you don't need more dashboards — you need clarity that connects governance to business results.

The scorecard helps you:

- Track whether visibility governance is being operationalized
- Identify accountability gaps and bottlenecks
- Demonstrate ROI from structural improvements
- Align finance, IT, and marketing around visibility equity

Treat this as a recurring part of leadership and board reporting — not a one-off audit.

Who Owns the Scorecard

Ownership should sit at the intersection of marketing, finance, and technology — typically the CMO or CDO.

However:

The senior SEO or visibility leader must be a standing contributor.

They understand technical dependencies, recovery timelines, and revenue exposure better than anyone else.

GOVERNANCE AND VISIBILITY MATURITY SCORECARD

Rate each dimension quarterly on a 1–5 scale:

(1 = emerging, 5 = optimized)

1. Strategic Integration

- SEO and visibility explicitly referenced in corporate strategy
- Visibility metrics included in board materials
- Cross-functional leadership owns results collaboratively

Ask yourself:

Do leaders view visibility as a growth engine — or still as a marketing tactic?

2. Governance Infrastructure

- Policies exist for SEO, accessibility, and AI content governance
- CMS and deployment workflows enforce quality gates
- External audits verify compliance annually

Ask yourself:

Would a regulator view your governance as credible?

3. Financial Stewardship

- SEO funded as a multi-year investment, not campaign spend
- Shared dashboards reveal true search ROI: organic + paid
- Savings from reduced paid-media dependency reinvested in capability

Ask yourself:

Is SEO treated as infrastructure — or a discretionary cost?

4. Cross-Functional Execution

- IT, Product, Marketing, and Compliance review visibility together
- Decisions affecting discoverability are documented and governed

- AI-assisted outputs verified by humans before publication

Ask yourself:

Do teams protect visibility collaboratively — or weaken it in silos?

5. Culture and Capability

- Governance influences KPIs — including executive scorecards
- Skills uplift driven by recurring training and refresh cycles
- Employees clearly understand how their role affects search trust

Ask yourself:

Is governance embedded in culture — or only performed when prompted?

IMPLEMENTING THE EXECUTIVE REVIEW CYCLE

Quarterly Review

- Include visibility metrics in board packets
- Invite the senior SEO executive to report status and risk
- Escalate declines in maturity immediately
- Validate budget continuity for oversight and capability
- Celebrate improvements — they reinforce desired behavior

Annual Benchmark

- Track visibility equity YoY (organic market share)
- Review audit results, governance adherence, and technical health
- Prioritize next-year investment using maturity trends
- Publish a short visibility governance outcomes report internally

Recognition and Accountability

- Recognize governance improvement publicly
- Tie visibility objectives to leadership KPIs
- Make compliance and regression prevention visible in performance reviews
- Ensure that knowledge retention survives personnel turnover

EXECUTIVE GOVERNANCE CHECKLIST: REVIEW CADENCE

Quarterly

☐ Review visibility governance at the board level

☐ Confirm automation risks are monitored and escalated

☐ Require written executive sign-off on visibility KPIs

☐ Ensure talent continuity for SEO and analytics

☐ Protect visibility during reorgs, CMS change, and vendor shifts

Annually

☐ Commission independent audits of accessibility and SEO

☐ Assess multi-year ROI of organic vs. paid acquisition

☐ Refresh AI governance policies and controls

☐ Fund ongoing capability uplift (people + processes + compliance)

☐ Publish a Digital Integrity and Discoverability Statement

Example Digital Integrity and Discoverability Statement

Search visibility and digital trust are strategic assets for our organization. We are committed to ensuring that every stakeholder—customers, regulators, and partners—can reliably find accurate content that reflects who we are and what we offer.

To support this, we uphold enterprise governance across five key dimensions:

- Accuracy and consistency of digital information across all channels
- Accessibility that meets and advances recognized standards
- AI governance that preserves brand integrity and prevents automation errors
- Structured data and metadata standards that enable machine understanding
- Cross-functional accountability for performance and risk management

We monitor our visibility performance quarterly and validate governance maturity through annual independent audits.

Our ambition is to deliver discoverability with integrity—to ensure we are findable for the right reasons, in the right moments, in the right places.

LEADERSHIP REFLECTION

Governance maturity is not perfection — it is **predictability**.

When you treat visibility as infrastructure — not as a campaign or a marketing project — discoverability becomes reliable, capability becomes transferable, and your entire digital presence becomes investor-ready.

The scorecard is your instrument panel.

Your organization is the engine.

When both stay aligned, visibility becomes not just strong — but sustainable.

Chapter 10

SECURING FUNDING AND
SUSTAINING GOVERNANCE

Executive Summary

Visibility is an appreciating asset — until the funding stops.

This chapter shows you how to secure durable investment for search visibility and governance maturity by reframing SEO from a monthly cost into a resilience-building capability.

Your responsibility is to ensure discoverability is not a "nice to have" that gets cut first, but a protected pillar of trust and growth.

If AI assistants can't find you, neither will customers — obtain the budget needed to protect your visibility.

WHY VISIBILITY NEEDS RELIABLE FUNDING

Annual budget cycles often treat SEO like a campaign. But visibility doesn't thrive in bursts — it compounds through steady investment.

The most damaging mindset is:

"We'll reinvest when we see more results."

Yet SEO results *are* the reinvestment. When funding pauses, organic visibility fades; paid acquisition rises to compensate; and margins quietly erode.

Like skipping preventive maintenance, the damage becomes visible only when recovery is most expensive.

FRAMING SEO AS AN ASSET — NOT A COST

Executives invest confidently in three things:

1. **Assets** that appreciate,

2. **Capabilities** that improve efficiency, and

3. **Systems** that reduce risk.

SEO qualifies as all three.

Instead of saying, "We need $250K for SEO,"

say,

"We will protect $8M in recurring revenue with a $250K visibility-equity investment."

Funding must follow contribution. If organic search drives 40% of revenue, it deserves more than 4% of the budget.

(For financial governance frameworks and ROI tracking methods, see Chapter 6.)

WHY SEO BUDGETS GET CUT FIRST

Budget visibility disappears first because it is misunderstood, and possibly because no one consulted the responsible SEO manager before the decision was made.

Executives often assume SEO is "free," dashboards lag, and no single department defends the line item. Your job is to make organic revenue exposure impossible to ignore.

Blind-Spot Check

If your visibility funding can be cut without triggering a risk review, you are governing a cost, not an asset.

Funding Visibility as a Long-Horizon Control System

Visibility investments fail most often not because the strategy is wrong, but because visibility funding is treated as discretionary. In many organizations, SEO, content integrity, and AI readiness are funded opportunistically—**expanded during growth cycles and trimmed at the first sign of pressure.** This stop-start pattern quietly undermines governance.

Machine-mediated discovery systems reward **consistency over bursts**. Authority, entity strength, and citation reliability accumulate through sustained signals—stable publishing standards, durable structured data, disciplined updates, and continuity of expertise. When funding fluctuates, those signals fragment. The result is not an immediate collapse, but a gradual erosion that only becomes visible once recovery is expensive and slow.

Executives often ask for short-term proof before committing long-term funding. In AI-mediated search, that logic reverses cause and effect. You do not fund visibility because results are guaranteed; you fund it because **withdrawal creates asymmetric downside**. Once an organization disappears from synthesized answers or recommendation sets, regaining inclusion can take quarters—even if spending later increases.

Governance reframes the funding question. Instead of asking whether visibility "paid off" last quarter, leadership asks whether the organization maintained eligibility for discovery across changing systems. This shifts funding from performance marketing to **risk prevention and capability insurance**, similar to cybersecurity or regulatory compliance.

Strategic patience is therefore not passive. It is an active governance choice to protect continuity:

- Stable funding preserves signal coherence across algorithm changes.
- Predictable investment supports institutional knowledge and specialist retention.
- Long-horizon budgets allow controlled experimentation without jeopardizing core visibility.

When visibility funding is governed rather than debated annually, organizations stop oscillating between urgency and neglect. They maintain presence while competitors churn. Over time, this patience compounds into an advantage—not because spending is higher, but because interruption never occurs.

For boards, the implication is straightforward: **visibility cannot be governed if it is not funded predictably**. Treating discovery as infrastructure—rather than a campaign—aligns investment with the timeframes that AI systems actually reward.

GOVERNANCE BUILDS FUNDING CONFIDENCE

Boards don't fear spending; they fear *uncontrolled* spending.

When governance demonstrates clear ownership, early-warning indicators, and quantifiable results, funding becomes defensible.

The dashboards and audit systems described in Chapter 8 make this accountability visible, converting uncertainty into confidence.

HOW TO PRESENT A BUSINESS CASE THAT WINS

A persuasive visibility proposal fits on one page:

Objective: Protect and grow recurring revenue through visibility infrastructure.

Investment: Technical SEO, content governance, and platform stability.

ROI: Compounding returns, reduced CAC, and risk mitigation.

Risk of Underfunding: Loss of organic share → rising paid dependency → EBITDA erosion.

Executives approve what they can explain to the board in one sentence.

Frame your proposal as *revenue protection*, not marketing expansion.

FUNDING MODELS THAT SURVIVE ECONOMIC PRESSURE

Financial resilience depends on structure, not enthusiasm.

Sustainable funding models include:

- **Multi-year capital planning:** Treat SEO infrastructure as amortizable digital property.
- **Paid-to-organic reinvestment:** Redirect a portion of paid-media efficiency gains to strengthen visibility.
- **Risk-adjusted budgets:** Fund visibility protection like insurance — steady and preventive.

This shifts SEO from:

Operational expense → **Enterprise infrastructure**

Marketing line item → **Long-term asset**

The next emerging funding challenge comes not from finance departments, but from algorithms.

DISCOVERABILITY RISK — BEING OVERLOOKED BY MACHINES

As AI-driven agents increasingly act on behalf of customers, search visibility is no longer just about being *seen* — it's about being *selected*.

Algorithms decide which brands appear first, often without a human ever viewing a results page.

Executives must assume that automated systems will:

- Default to the most structured, current information.
- Prefer brands that demonstrate authority and consistency.
- Filter out outdated or conflicting content automatically.

This creates **selection risk** — exclusion by systems, not by customers.

To counter this, ensure continuous:

- Metadata and schema discipline across all digital assets.
- Monitoring of accuracy in data feeds, pricing, and product data.
- Governance oversight of how AI systems describe and cite your business.

(For detailed AI automation governance controls, see Chapter 5.)

Measurement Alert

Visibility isn't enough — systems must *choose* you, even when users never see the list of options.

CHANGE MANAGEMENT WITHOUT REGRESSION

When organizations restructure, visibility often loses a champion.

Executives should mandate that visibility, ownership, and capability continuity persist through every change event.

Governance requirements:

- Maintain SEO accountability within all transformation programs.
- Protect redirects, schema markup, internal links, and authoritative legacy content.
- Enforce mandatory SEO sign-off for CMS or platform changes.
- Retain access credentials for Search Console, analytics, and reporting systems.

Change is inevitable; regression is optional.

(For operational change-control frameworks, see Chapter 6.)

BOARD-LEVEL QUESTIONS TO SECURE SUSTAINABLE FUNDING

Review these quarterly:

- Is SEO funded in proportion to the revenue at stake?
- Do visibility KPIs appear in board materials?
- Is one leader accountable for cross-functional outcomes?
- Are paid costs rising faster than total search revenue?
- Do governance alerts escalate promptly to executives?

If any answer is *no*, your funding — and your visibility — are exposed.

FUNDING AND INVESTMENT CHECKLIST

- ☐ Align budget scale to organic revenue exposure.
- ☐ Maintain visibility as a recurring board agenda item.

☐ Require SEO involvement in all transformation initiatives.

☐ Allocate multi-year visibility funding.

☐ Tie governance outcomes to leadership scorecards.

☐ Reinvest paid-efficiency gains into visibility capability.

You don't need to master the tags—you need to protect the capability that keeps your customers on your path.

LEADERSHIP REFLECTION

The companies that thrive aren't those that spend the most on visibility — but those that never have to buy back the visibility they once earned.

When you treat discoverability as:

- Infrastructure,
- Risk insurance, and
- Brand equity,
- performance becomes predictable and revenue resilient.

FROM FUNDING RESILIENCE TO LEADERSHIP CONTINUITY

Securing funding protects visibility today; sustaining leadership behavior protects it tomorrow.

Budgets and governance frameworks can preserve discoverability only as long as leadership attention remains constant.

The next chapter moves from financial discipline to organizational discipline—how visible organizations stay ahead by embedding visibility governance into culture, operations, and executive behavior.

Chapter 11

HOW VISIBLE ORGANIZATIONS STAY AHEAD

EXECUTIVE SUMMARY

Discoverability is not luck; it is a competitive discipline governed over time.

This chapter equips you with the leadership mindset and operating habits that set digitally mature organizations apart from those that constantly react to algorithm changes, restructurings, and rising acquisition costs. In mature organizations, visibility is treated as governed infrastructure, not a tactical output.

Your role now is to ensure that the systems, people, and governance structures responsible for discoverability remain effective regardless of platform shifts, leadership change, or automation.

WHY LEADERSHIP MATTERS MOST NOW

Most visibility failures are not technical failures. They are leadership and governance failures.

Organizations that remain consistently visible do so because leadership ensures continuity of governance even as tools, teams, and channels evolve. Leaders who succeed:

- Maintain continuity in visibility governance through leadership change

- Demand cross-functional accountability through formal governance structures
- Invest in resilience before a crisis forces reactive spending
- Align objectives across digital, product, content, and customer functions

Leaders who struggle tend to act only after visibility has already disappeared from dashboards, when recovery is slow, expensive, and often incomplete.

In VGMM terms, this is the difference between visibility that depends on individuals and visibility that persists as an organizational capability.

VISIBILITY AS STRATEGIC INSURANCE

Organic and AI-mediated visibility protects revenue when:

- Paid budgets are reduced
- Algorithms and ranking systems change
- Products, positioning, or messaging pivot
- Markets contract or competition intensifies

Organizations that remain discoverable through disruption maintain profit efficiency, while competitors increasingly rely on paid channels to compensate for lost organic and AI-mediated presence. Over time, this resilience supports valuation by reducing dependency on variable acquisition costs.

Visibility resilience is business resilience.

HOW HIGH-PERFORMING ORGANIZATIONS OPERATE

High-performing organizations follow a repeatable governance playbook rather than relying on individual expertise or heroics. In these organizations:

- Visibility governance is enforced at the system level, not the team level
- Visibility KPIs sit alongside revenue, risk, and resilience metrics
- SEO and AI visibility representation is included early in roadmap and product decisions
- Workforce changes do not disrupt capability or institutional knowledge
- CMS, platform, and architectural decisions require discoverability sign-off
- Automation is supervised through governance rather than trusted unquestioningly
- Successful practices are institutionalized as standards, not one-off wins

These organizations treat visibility governance maturity, as defined in the VGMM, as an operating requirement rather than a maturity aspiration.

They also formalize decision-making through a Visibility Governance Committee (VGC), so visibility risks, trade-offs, and exceptions are resolved through documented decision rights rather than hallway negotiations.

POSITIONING THE SEO FUNCTION AND GIVING IT A VOICE

Technology and process alone cannot protect visibility if accountability sits too low in the organization.

Even highly capable SEO teams cannot influence product, design, or infrastructure decisions unless visibility governance has formal executive-level authority. In mature organizations, SEO is a governed capability within visibility governance, and the VGC is the escalation forum when discoverability conflicts with speed, design, compliance, or platform constraints.

In mature organizations, SEO does not operate in isolation; it functions as a governed capability within a broader visibility governance system that also includes content, performance, accessibility, analytics, and AI-mediated representation.

Elevating SEO Requires Executive Sponsorship

Visibility works as intended only when senior leadership treats it as strategic infrastructure rather than a marketing accessory.

When executives elevate visibility governance within the organizational structure, communication between product, marketing, technology, and compliance improves naturally. Discoverability becomes a shared responsibility governed through the Visibility Governance Committee (VGC), rather than negotiated informally after launch.

When visibility leadership briefs decision-makers early, conflicts are resolved before release, and collaboration replaces post-launch remediation.

Positioning and Accountability

By this point, it should be clear that visibility governance warrants direct executive oversight.

Visibility influences revenue, margin, risk, and competitive positioning across industries, particularly in ecommerce and digital-first businesses. Yet many organizations still position SEO as a downstream activity rather than an upstream governance input.

A commonly shared web-design workflow diagram illustrates this misunderstanding.

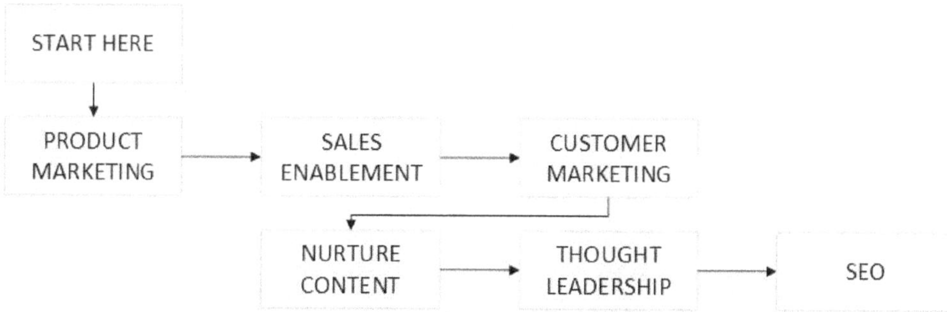

Figure 7 Not where I would position the SEO input.

SEO is not a final step after thought leadership has been executed. Effective workflows begin with product management sharing vision, market positioning, and personas with visibility teams before design or content production begins.

When SEO and visibility specialists return with researched entities, terminology, and demand signals, content teams can produce assets aligned with how search engines and AI systems interpret relevance.

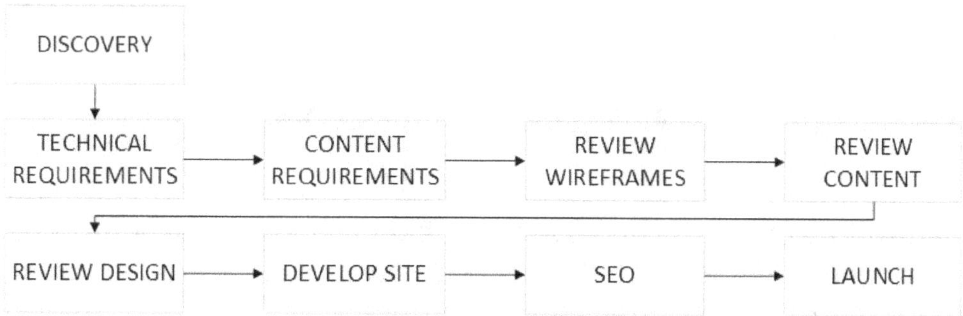

Figure 8 SEO was late to this party.

Someone suggested a minor modification to the diagram above to illustrate their experience.

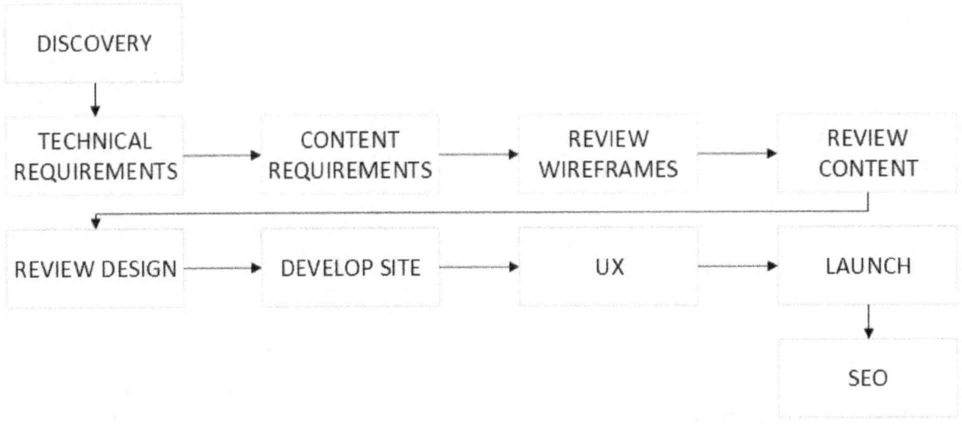

Figure 9 Another example of SEO input after the launch.

These diagrams reflect two unresolved questions:

- Which function owns accountability for visibility governance?
- At what level of seniority does that accountability sit?

Without formal governance and executive sponsorship, visibility remains reactive rather than strategic.

WHY ORGANIZATIONS RELEARN VISIBILITY LESSONS

Most visibility failures are not caused by ignorance. They are caused by organizational memory loss. These artifacts are owned and enforced through the VGC and treated as maturity controls in the VGMM, so they survive reorganizations and vendor changes.

Organizations repeatedly rediscover the same truths:

- Visibility collapses during platform migrations
- Content quality erodes when ownership diffuses
- Discoverability declines when experienced specialists leave

- AI systems misrepresent brands when governance lapses

These lessons are learned, documented, and briefly acted upon, only to be forgotten as leadership changes or priorities shift. The cycle repeats because knowledge of visibility resides in people, not in governed systems.

High-performing organizations break this cycle by institutionalizing visibility memory through governance artifacts defined and maintained by the VGC:

- Mandatory pre-release checks for discoverability impact
- Post-incident reviews when rankings, coverage, or AI citations regress
- Standing executive agenda items where visibility risk is reviewed alongside revenue and security
- Living documentation aligned with VGMM maturity targets that survives team turnover

Without this institutional memory, every leadership transition resets understanding to zero. New executives ask why SEO "suddenly became important again." New teams repeat preventable mistakes. Visibility debt accumulates invisibly until it becomes expensive or irreversible.

AI-mediated discovery increases the cost of forgetting. When organizations lose consistency—terminology, entity definitions, content standards—machines do not pause to wait for internal alignment. They substitute another source. Recovery requires rebuilding trust signals that were once taken for granted.

Executives often assume maturity is permanent. In reality, visibility maturity declines without reinforcement. Governance is the mechanism that arrests this decay. It ensures that hard-won insights are preserved as rules, workflows, and escalation paths—not anecdotes shared at offsites.

Visible organizations stay ahead not because they are smarter, but because they remember. They treat discovery lessons the way safety-critical industries treat incidents: as institutional knowledge that must never be relearned the hard way.

The leadership responsibility is clear. If visibility knowledge is not embedded in governance, it will be lost in the next reorganization—and the organization will pay to rediscover it.

THE MARKETING FUNNEL AND LEADERSHIP OVERSIGHT

SEO and AI-mediated visibility operate across the entire marketing funnel, from initial discovery through evaluation and conversion.

Tactical mapping of keywords and content to funnel stages is covered in Book 2, *Accidental SEO Manager*. At the executive level, the responsibility is to ensure that visibility governance spans all funnel stages, receives sustained funding, and is measured by business outcomes rather than isolated rankings.

Real-Life Examples

On Facebook and Twitter, I once asked the following question:

Ash Nallawalla
9 April at 07:21

I notice that in North America, SEO sits in the Marketing department, while in Australia, it sits on the "Product" side, which can go by various names, but essentially, "not Marketing". In fact, I have been in three companies, where (before I got there) SEO was taken out of Marketing.

Is this an accurate observation? I would also like to hear about the positioning in other countries.

Figure 10 Where does SEO sit in your company?

Here are some replies (redacted for privacy):

- "It's not uncommon to be in marketing, but also not unusual not to be."
- "In Europe, SEO is also a part of the marketing department."
- "In the U.S., I've seen SEO report to IT, Marketing, Sales, and directly to the C-suite — no one can agree where SEO lies."
- "The best place for it to lie is where it will get the most respect and the recommendations will be carried out."
- "On one side of our organization, SEO reports to marketing, and on the other side, to IT."
- "When I worked at XYZ, they had SEOs in two different departments — neither was a traditional marketing group."

Other professions have well-defined reporting lines.

Electronic engineers never report into marketing.

Software developers do not report to finance.

So why is the visibility reporting chain so complex?

SEARCH MARKETING — STRATEGIC INTEGRATION

Executives should view SEO and paid search as complementary components of a unified search-marketing strategy.

Tactical distinctions between channels are covered in Book 2, *Accidental SEO Manager*.

At the leadership level, the priority is to align budgets, teams, and KPIs so that both organic and paid search support shared business goals.

Job Titles and Career Path

Let's begin finding a home for this orphan team, starting with some job titles. The titles below are grouped into two categories: those who know very little about SEO but have that responsibility assigned to them, and the SEO operative titles.

Accountability Titles

In most large companies, SEO responsibility is given to roles such as:

- Executive Manager
- General Manager
- VP Online Sales
- Chief Marketing Officer
- Managing Director
- Marketing Director
- Marketing Manager
- Manager, Digital Marketing
- Ecommerce Manager
- IT Manager

In smaller organizations:

- CEO
- Sales Manager
- Marketing Manager

Responsibility often follows the person who champions the role, not a defined structure.

Operative Titles

Operatives are the practitioners who optimize sites day-to-day. A structured career path can help retain talent and build maturity:

- Junior SEO
- SEO Specialist
- Senior SEO Specialist

- SEO Lead
- Technical SEO
- Senior Technical SEO
- SEO Manager
- SEO Director
- Chief Visibility Officer (CVO)
- VP of Visibility

It's heartening to see on LinkedIn that a few people have their title as Chief Visibility Officer.

ELEVATING THE SEO FUNCTION

True maturity comes when executives view SEO leadership as integral to corporate governance, not an optional marketing task.

In a perfect world, where should SEO sit?

It certainly does not belong in Technology, though there is a tussle between Sales, Product, and Marketing.

I would place it in Marketing, not Sales.

Marketing generally receives the largest budgets with the least resistance, making it easier to embed SEO funding.

The Product and Sales verticals often struggle to secure long-term SEO investment.

Chief Visibility Officer

In a large company, visibility leadership belongs in the C-suite.

I recommend the **Chief Visibility Officer (CVO)** title, positioned alongside the CMO and CIO, and compensated accordingly.

The CVO's responsibility is *to maximize visibility and online conversions* through effective governance, infrastructure, and collaboration.

When performance drops, the CEO calls the CVO first. The CVO sponsors the VGC to ensure visibility decisions are enforceable across product, marketing, engineering, content, analytics, and risk.

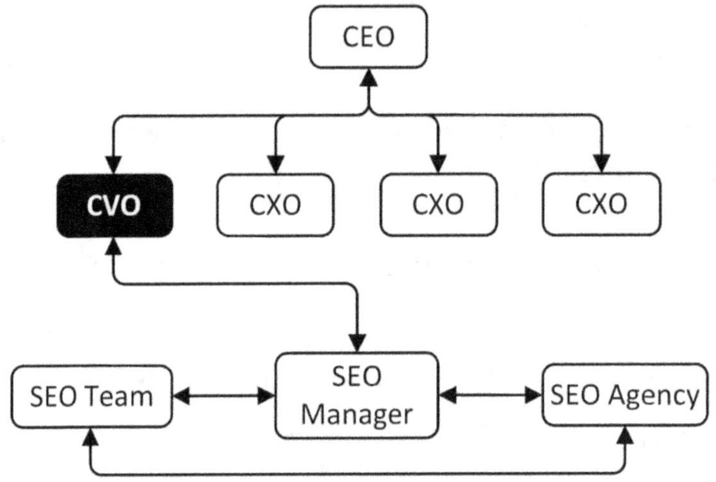

Figure 11 Positioning the Chief Visibility Officer (CVO) and the SEO team.

Core Responsibilities

- Maximizing digital visibility
- Maximizing online conversions
- Visibility governance
- Operations and maintenance
- Managing website teams

The intranet should also be managed by the same group, even though HR or other departments may own the content.

The CVO does not decide which hardware to procure for the website, but the CIO is more likely to listen to the CVO team's input than under the old approach.

Teams reporting to the CVO typically include:

- SEO Team
- Web/App Developers and Platform Engineers
- Designers
- Analytics and CRO Specialists
- CMS and Content Teams
- UX and Accessibility Teams

This configuration consolidates accountability for digital performance under a single leadership point.

An Independent Website Team

If you cannot create a CVO role, build an independent website team separate from internal silos.

This group operates like a small in-house agency, with the autonomy to address urgent SEO and visibility issues without bureaucratic friction.

Adopt a Single-Threaded Leader (STL) model, as championed by Amazon — one leader with authority and accountability focused solely on the website's success.

The independence of this team is not about isolation — it's about ensuring that visibility decisions reach leadership without distortion.

STRUCTURED SEO IN COMPANY-WIDE WORKFLOWS

SEO principles must be embedded in company workflows, not confined to a department.

Designers should build for accessibility; developers should maintain performance standards; compliance teams should audit structured data periodically.

Regular SEO audits can verify that all departments remain aligned with discoverability principles.

Culture, Collaboration, and Trust

Corporate silos often evolve into "islands of excellence"—efficient within themselves but disconnected from one another.

Digital transformation succeeds only when cutting-edge teams blend with legacy silos through collaboration and mutual trust.

I have seen design teams conduct usability tests with too few participants, drawing sweeping conclusions, or IT departments deploy updates that inadvertently break key SEO elements.

All were well-intentioned but costly to fix later.

If SEO is seen as a blocker, it's often because leadership hasn't modeled collaboration.

Include SEO in planning meetings early — even as optional invitees.

Awareness itself prevents regressions.

"The key there is to make sure executives understand that SEO isn't supposed to be a tactic: it's supposed to be a culture."

— Stephan Bajaio

When the C-suite owns visibility within the organizational culture, SEO becomes a trusted interpreter of customer intent—not a messenger of bad news.

SEO is digital visibility insurance: protection for how your brand is found, represented, and trusted.

When executives recognize that, communication improves, silos weaken, and discoverability becomes predictable.

THE VISIBILITY CULTURE SHIFT

With the right structure in place, culture follows.

In mature organizations:

- SEO is not "marketing work" — it is business continuity
- Speed and governance reinforce each other, not compete
- Accessibility and structured data are part of quality standards
- Executives celebrate accuracy and relevance — not just volume

Visibility becomes everyone's responsibility — and no one's surprise.

Detecting Visibility Drift Before Performance Declines

High-performing organizations do not wait for rankings or revenue to fall before intervening. They monitor for visibility drift—**the gradual misalignment between how the organization intends to be represented and how search and AI systems actually present it.**

Visibility drift often appears long before performance metrics change. It shows up as subtle inconsistencies:

- AI summaries emphasizing outdated positioning
- Product comparisons omitting differentiators that leadership believes are core
- Increased reliance on paid channels to sustain stable outcomes
- Content teams publishing material that is technically correct but strategically misaligned
- Structured data coverage lagging behind product or policy changes

These signals rarely trigger alarms in traditional dashboards. They surface only when leadership actively inspects representation, not just results.

Mature organizations institutionalize this inspection. They treat external representation as something to review rather than as a given. Executives periodically ask:

"How are we being described right now by systems we do not control?"

The answer often surprises them.

This inspection is not a marketing exercise. It is a governance function. Just as financial controls detect variance before losses compound, visibility inspection detects narrative and eligibility drift before discoverability erodes.

Organizations that stay ahead do three things consistently:

- They review AI-mediated summaries of their brand and competitors at set intervals
- They compare intended positioning with surfaced positioning
- They assign ownership for correcting gaps, not debating whether they matter

When visibility drift is treated as an operational risk, corrective action happens early and quietly. When it is ignored, recovery becomes expensive, public, and reactive.

Sustained visibility leadership is not about constant optimization. It is about preventing silent divergence between strategy and machine interpretation.

WHAT BOARDS SHOULD MONITOR CONTINUOUSLY

Boards should treat drops in visibility like financial risk, not marketing volatility.

Key indicators include:

- Organic share of revenue vs. paid dependency.

- Governance exceptions unresolved beyond two weeks.
- Capability concentration — more than one person required to safeguard visibility.
- Cross-functional process adherence.
- Technical health of templates and architecture.
- Impacts of restructures or vendor transitions.

These indicators are also maturity signals. If they are not reviewed consistently, the organization is drifting down the VGMM scale even if performance appears stable.

Visibility Must Survive Leadership Change

Most visibility failures do not occur during crises. They occur during **leadership transitions**.

When a new CEO, CMO, or CIO arrives, priorities reset. Budgets are re-examined. Reporting lines shift. In that turbulence, visibility often loses its sponsor—not because anyone disagrees with its importance, but because no one at the top explicitly owns it.

Search visibility is unusually vulnerable right now. It is:

- Cross-functional
- Long-horizon
- Technically mediated
- Poorly understood outside specialist teams

As a result, it is easy for new leaders to treat it as inherited noise rather than strategic infrastructure. Measurement gets simplified. Dashboards disappear. Investment pauses "until we reassess." Six to twelve months later, performance decays—but the cause is no longer visible.

High-performing organizations design for leadership turnover. They assume executives will change, and they **anchor visibility accountability to governance, not personalities**.

The VGC provides **continuity of oversight**, and the VGMM provides **continuity of expectations**, so visibility does not need to be re-argued every time executives change.

This shows up in three ways.

First, visibility is embedded into board-level review cycles, not as a marketing update, but as a standing item alongside risk, margin, and technology resilience. New executives inherit the expectation that discoverability is monitored, not optional.

Second, decision rights are documented. It is always clear:

- Who approves changes that affect crawlability, structure, or automation
- Who owns AI representation risk
- Who is accountable when visibility degrades, regardless of cause

Third, visibility maturity targets extend beyond the individual level. The organization knows what "good" looks like and tracks drift when leadership changes. Progress is not reset simply because someone new is in the role.

AI-mediated discovery increases the importance of this continuity. LLMs do not care about executive reshuffles. They react to inconsistency immediately. When content standards slip or authority signals weaken, substitution happens quietly—and often permanently.

Boards should therefore treat visibility continuity as they do financial controls and cybersecurity posture. It must survive a leadership change without renegotiation.

The ultimate blind spot is assuming that visibility will take care of itself once it has been "fixed." In reality, visibility is a living asset. Without executive continuity, it erodes. Without governance, it disappears.

Visible organizations stay ahead because leadership change does not reset their discoverability. The system holds—no matter who is in the chair.

THE ROLE OF AI IN FUTURE VISIBILITY

Search, recommendation, and conversational systems now mediate how customers encounter your brand.

To surface consistently, leadership must ensure that:

- Data and content are structured for machine interpretation.
- Brand representations in AI tools are supervised for accuracy.
- Internal knowledge remains indexable by authorized models.
- Governance policies address AI-generated summaries and responses.

Your visibility now depends as much on what **machines infer** as on what **humans see**.

TREND ALERT — AGENTIC BROWSERS AND AI DISCOVERY

The next wave of digital discovery is already here: AI-driven browsers and personal agents that search, evaluate, and act on behalf of users. These systems will determine which brands are chosen — often without a human ever clicking a result.

For executives, the implications are clear:

- Visibility metrics must evolve from clicks to selection by agents.

- Websites must be machine-ready, not only human-friendly — rich structured data, stable APIs, and governance over how agents access assets.
- Governance teams must anticipate agent-driven risks: brand representation, inclusion/exclusion decisions, and unauthorized summarization.

Failing to adapt to this shift may keep traffic stable but quietly erode influence and margin.

(For technical readiness guidance, see Chapter 5: *AI and Automation — New Governance Imperatives.*)

AI Visibility as an Early Warning System

High-performing organizations do not wait for revenue decline to signal trouble. They detect weak signals upstream—before demand shifts appear in sales reports or dashboards.

AI-mediated visibility has become one such signal.

Because AI assistants continuously summarize markets, changes in how they describe your organization often precede measurable business impact. When AI systems start favoring alternative explanations, vendors, or solution framings, they are reflecting an underlying shift in perceived authority—even if customer behavior has not yet followed.

Executives in visible organizations monitor AI responses not for vanity, but for foresight.

They ask questions such as:

- Which competitors are now being named as default recommendations?
- Has our category framing changed in AI summaries?

- Are we still cited for strategic topics—or only for historical context?
- Are intermediaries replacing us as the authoritative source?

These shifts rarely appear in traditional metrics. They surface first in synthesized explanations, comparative answers, and advisory-style responses generated by AI systems.

Leading organizations treat these signals the way financial leaders treat credit spreads or inventory turns: as indicators of future movement, not present performance.

When AI systems begin to "explain the market" differently, executives take notice—because explanation precedes preference.

This is why advanced organizations institutionalize periodic AI visibility reviews at the leadership level. The reviews are scheduled, documented, and escalated through the VGC when representation drift, exclusion, or competitive displacement is observed.

They do not outsource interpretation. They treat AI-mediated perception as a strategic input into planning, positioning, and risk management.

Visibility leadership means recognizing that the future market often shows up first in how machines talk about you—long before customers do.

THE STRATEGIC IMPERATIVE OF OWNED CHANNELS

Having established strong search and AI visibility governance, mature organizations face a strategic question: how to reduce dependency on platforms they don't control. Search engines and AI systems represent the largest share of digital discovery for most organizations. However, boards must acknowledge a fundamental limitation: **you do not control these platforms**.

As organic search traffic continues its structural decline—accelerated by zero-click behavior and AI-mediated answers—leading organizations are shifting capital allocation toward channels they own: social platforms, direct marketing, experiential events, gaming environments, virtual experiences, and audience-building mechanisms that create direct relationships independent of algorithmic intermediation.

This is not a retreat from SEO. It is a strategic rebalancing. The ultimate visibility strategy is to extract value from platforms you cannot control while systematically reducing dependency on them. Organizations that maintain strong search governance while simultaneously investing in **owned** audience channels position themselves for resilience across multiple discovery modes.

Strategic Considerations for Boards

The decision to diversify beyond search dependency requires board-level attention because the investment thesis differs fundamentally from traditional marketing spend:

Owned channels behave like capital assets. An invested audience—subscribers, community members, registered users, event participants—creates compounding value over time. Unlike paid search, where budget cessation causes immediate visibility loss, owned audiences provide durable reach that appreciates with **engagement**.

Industry context determines relevance. Not every organization benefits equally from all owned channels. A B2B manufacturer may find trade events and technical communities more strategic than TikTok or VR experiences. Consumer brands targeting younger demographics face the opposite calculus. Boards should demand audience strategies aligned with customer behavior, not platform novelty.

Search governance enables owned channel investment.
Counterintuitively, strong visibility governance *frees* resources for
audience building. When search becomes predictable baseline hygiene
rather than a perpetual crisis, marketing budgets can shift toward
owned channels without abandoning discovery infrastructure.

The Emerging Duopoly

Marketing leaders increasingly describe a **visibility duopoly**: "Google-
sourced traffic" versus "everything else." In this framing, search and AI
platforms represent **rented visibility**—valuable but inherently
unstable and subject to algorithmic changes outside organizational
control. Owned channels represent **acquired visibility**—harder to build
but more defensible once established.

The governance structures discussed throughout this book support
both strategies. They ensure that search visibility does not deteriorate
due to neglect as leadership attention shifts to audience ownership.
They prevent the costly mistake of abandoning discovery
infrastructure in pursuit of owned channels, only to discover that
owned audiences still require search visibility to grow efficiently.

Board Action Framework

Boards should evaluate their organization's **visibility portfolio** using
the following criteria:

- What percentage of inbound demand originates from owned
  versus rented channels? Track this mix over time to understand
  strategic exposure.
- Are owned channel investments treated as capital assets with
  multi-year ROI expectations? Audience building requires
  patient capital that survives quarterly pressure.
- Does the organization maintain search governance maturity
  while diversifying discovery channels? Degrading search

infrastructure to fund owned channels often proves counterproductive.

- Is industry context reflected in channel selection? Avoid platform-chasing that ignores customer behavior patterns specific to your sector.

The governance frameworks in this book remain essential even as organizations reduce their reliance on search. Visibility failures in search and AI systems create downstream damage that affects owned channel performance—poor search results undermine brand trust, indexation problems create attribution gaps, and AI misrepresentation shapes perceptions that owned channels must then correct.

This book addresses search and AI visibility governance because these surfaces remain mission-critical for most organizations. The strategic shift toward owned channels does not eliminate the need for visibility discipline—it underscores the importance of maintaining search as a baseline channel. At the same time, capital flows toward channels that offer greater strategic control.

For organizations where owned channels represent core strategy— gaming publishers, social platforms, event producers, membership organizations—the principles of governance, measurement, and accountability discussed here apply directly to those channels as well. The underlying discipline remains constant even as the surfaces change.

WHEN YOU KNOW VISIBILITY THINKING HAS TAKEN HOLD

You'll notice cultural markers such as:

- SEO and accessibility checks occur proactively.
- Product and content teams consult SEO early.
- Visibility regressions trigger action, not argument.

- Financial planning includes organic revenue protection.
- Decisions consider how customers and algorithms interpret the brand.

At this stage, SEO has evolved from a repair function to a strategic competency.

ORGANIZATIONAL EXCELLENCE AND LEADERSHIP CHECKLIST

- ☐ Review organic revenue exposure quarterly.

- ☐ Validate continuity of SEO leadership and skills.

- ☐ Require SEO involvement in digital transformation.

- ☐ Protect authoritative legacy content during migrations.

- ☐ Fund AI governance alongside visibility infrastructure.

- ☐ Celebrate governance achievements — not just acquisition results.

Your actions communicate priority far more clearly than any metric.

LEADERSHIP REFLECTION

Algorithms will evolve. Markets will change.

Your org charts will shift repeatedly.

The question isn't: "Can we regain visibility if we lose it?"

The leadership mandate is: "How do we ensure we never lose it?"

When visibility is governed as infrastructure, your organization remains discoverable — even when everything else moves.

FROM OPERATIONAL MASTERY TO LEADERSHIP VISION

When visibility governance becomes cultural, the next challenge isn't implementation — it's perspective.

The final chapter looks beyond dashboards, workflows, and budgets to the mindset that sustains them: an executive awareness that visibility is not about algorithms but alignment.

You've built the systems; now it's time to close the blind spot that obscures their true purpose—to make your organization findable, trusted, and accountable by design.

Chapter 12

EPILOGUE

CLOSING THE BLIND SPOT

If you've reached this point, you already see what most leaders don't: **visibility isn't about algorithms — it's about alignment.**

You close the blind spot not by learning SEO, but by empowering the people who practice it to shape the systems that define your organization's reach and reputation.

The work of governance doesn't end with policies, dashboards, or budgets. It ends when visibility is recognized as a signal of organizational health. When executives fund it with intent, measure it with rigor, and defend it with the same discipline they bring to finance, compliance, and risk.

Bring visibility into the boardroom.

Treat it as infrastructure, not initiative.

Make it as measurable — and as unmissable — as every other strategic asset.

YOU CAN'T MANAGE WHAT YOU CAN'T SEE

Across organizations large and small, search visibility — the single most public indicator of digital performance — remains hidden in the lower decks of marketing or IT.

This is the blind spot: an executive culture that prizes visibility in financial markets but overlooks it in the digital markets where customers actually find them.

When teams debate whether to fund "another SEO audit" or "a new analytics license," they're not arguing about marketing spend — they're arguing about discoverability.

Visibility isn't vanity; it's the currency of relevance.

Every search result, every app mention, every AI summary that includes or excludes your brand reflects decisions made months or years earlier — about governance, priority, and accountability.

FROM ACTIVITY TO ACCOUNTABILITY

Leaders who treat visibility as a line item will never own it.

Leaders who treat it as a signal of organizational health will make it a strength.

That difference — between activity and accountability — separates the visible from the forgotten.

In the AI era, visibility is no longer a marketing metric; it's an indicator of digital trust.

GOVERNANCE, TRUST, AND THE AI STANDARD

Search engines and AI models alike reward clarity, consistency, and structure — the same qualities that define well-governed enterprises.

When teams share metadata standards, content policies, and ethical AI practices, they're not just optimizing for algorithms; they're demonstrating the disciplined transparency that regulators, investors, and customers expect.

Agentic systems will continue to mediate attention; your governance maturity determines whether they mediate in your favor.

CLOSING THE BLIND SPOT BEGINS WITH LEADERSHIP VISION

Fund visibility, like fund risk management, should be systematic, with clear ownership, measurable outcomes, and direct executive oversight.

SEO is digital visibility insurance — the coverage that keeps you discoverable when everything else changes.

Empower your senior SEO or digital-visibility executive to collaborate at the level where strategy, technology, and brand intersect.

Their insight into how your organization appears — or fails to appear — is a proxy for how it actually operates.

Organizations that win in this new landscape won't just rank higher.

They'll show up better — everywhere that matters.

They'll be visible. They're coherent, trusted because they're consistent, and resilient because they're governed.

That's how you close the C-Suite Blind Spot — not by looking harder, but by leading smarter.

AUTHOR'S NOTE

When I wrote Book 2, *The Accidental SEO Manager*, I wanted to give overwhelmed professionals a map — a way to manage SEO without becoming a technician.

Each book since then has peeled back another layer of that same truth: visibility isn't a marketing trick; it's a management discipline.

Book 3, *AI Visibility Playbook*, explored how intelligent systems demand intelligent oversight.

Book 4: *Is Our SEO Working?* turned measurement into a mirror for organizational maturity.

This final volume, *The C-Suite Blind Spot*, asks leaders to look into that mirror and recognize visibility for what it is — **evidence of leadership clarity.**

If this series helps even one organization elevate its SEO and digital-governance conversations to the boardroom level, then the goal has been met.

Visibility is earned, but it's also enabled by executives who care enough to make it part of their culture.

Thank you for being one of them.

— Ash Nallawalla

Appendix A

VISIBILITY BLIND-SPOT AIDE-MEMOIRE

Quick checks for senior leaders

This aide-memoire summarizes the highest-impact risks that cause silent revenue leakage.
Use it in quarterly reviews and before any major change affecting the digital experience.

Leadership & Strategy Blind Spots

- You assume SEO is a marketing task — but visibility requires shared governance across Product, IT, Legal, Risk, and HR.
- You measure paid growth more than organic resilience — rising CAC may be masking visibility decay.
- You view SEO as a cost — instead of a compounding, depreciable asset generating future margin.

Leader question:

Who owns search visibility performance at the executive table?

Financial Blind Spots

- Organic revenue exposure is unknown or unreported.
- Short-term budget reallocations to paid search inflate CAC without growing share.
- Savings from improved visibility are not reinvested into content or infrastructure.

Leader question:

What would be the revenue impact if organic search declined 30% next quarter?

Technology Blind Spots

- Page speed regressions and indexation failures go unnoticed until traffic drops.
- Changes to templates or navigation remove structured data or internal links.
- Monitoring is reactive — failures appear in dashboards only after revenue loss.

Leader question:

Do platform changes require mandatory visibility sign-off before deployment?

Governance & Change-Management Blind Spots

- Restructures dilute SEO expertise and break accountability chains.
- New CMS deployments remove low-traffic pages that still carry authority.
- Product launches bypass redirects and accessibility baselines.

Leader question:

Is visibility risk reviewed before approving reorganizations or CMS migrations?

AI & Automation Blind Spots

- Generative content is published without human verification.
- Employees use unapproved AI tools that introduce compliance or brand risk.

- Discoverability governance is not integrated into AI governance reporting.

Leader question:

Who audits the decisions machines now make on your behalf?

Talent & Capability Blind Spots

- SEO skills reside in one or two individuals — key person risk.
- Data-literate and accessibility-aware talent is not being developed.
- No cross-training means solved problems get re-solved every time someone leaves.

Leader question:

How do we ensure visibility resilience when teams change?

Culture & Reporting Blind Spots

- Visibility metrics are not included in board discussions.
- Internal storytelling focuses on outputs (pages launched), not outcomes (equity gained).
- Governance performance is not tied to executive incentives.

Leader question:

Does visibility earn attention proportional to its contribution?

ONE-SLIDE BOARD REVIEW CONCLUSION

If any of these are true in your organization:

- Organic visibility share is declining
- Paid CAC is rising faster than revenue
- SEO responsibilities are unclear after the recent change

- Automation is deployed faster than oversight
- KPIs focus on activity rather than impact

...then you are **paying rent for customers you once owned**.

Executive Call to Action

Visibility is a fiduciary responsibility.
Protect it the way you protect finance, risk, and cybersecurity.

"Silent failures eventually become visible — in the P&L."

Appendix B

DIGITAL INTEGRITY & DISCOVERABILITY STATEMENT TEMPLATE

For annual stakeholder reporting

This template enables you to demonstrate visibility governance, content integrity, and resilience to stakeholders — including investors, regulators, and customers.

It positions discoverability and trust as measurable business outcomes.

This statement should be updated annually and endorsed by the C-suite sponsor.

Purpose of This Statement

To confirm that the organization:

- Protects its digital presence as a strategic asset
- Ensures content accuracy, accessibility, and visibility
- Governs automation and AI to uphold brand integrity
- Monitors discoverability as a leading indicator of trust and growth

Summary of Current Digital Integrity Health

Overall Rating:

★★★★★ (5-point maturity scale explained below)

The C-Suite Blind Spot

Scope of Review:

- Websites and digital products covered
- Regions and languages addressed

Key Strengths:

- Highest-performing visibility or governance capabilities

Improvement Priorities:

- Top risks and mitigation timelines

Visibility Governance Overview

Executive Ownership:

- Named sponsor (e.g., CMO, CDO, or Chief Visibility Officer)
- Senior SEO/visibility leader actively participates in executive reviews

Governance Controls in Place:

- Quarterly dashboards and risk escalations
- Pre-launch sign-off for SEO, accessibility, and compliance
- AI output oversight and audit trails

External Validation:

- Most recent SEO + external visibility audit date
- Summary of findings and compliance conformance

Performance Indicators

Visibility Equity

- Trend in organic share of search impressions and conversions
- Comparison with prior year and/or benchmark competitors

Technical Health

- % of pages passing Core Web Vitals
- Indexation, accessibility, and schema completeness trends

Content Integrity

- % content accuracy reviews completed
- Policy compliance for AI-generated material

Risk Management

- Count and severity of governance exceptions
- Resolution rate and regression prevention

Maturity Ratings

- **5 Optimized** — Governance fully embedded and continuously improving
- **4 Mature** — Sustained performance with proactive risk reduction
- **3 Developing** — Solid operation, but visibility reliant on key individuals
- **2 Emerging** — Inconsistent controls and reactive problem-solving
- **1 Vulnerable** — High dependency on paid channels and fragile processes

Leadership Commentary

Short narrative (300–500 words) summarizing:

- How governance improvements strengthened stakeholder trust
- How visibility performance supported revenue growth and efficiency

The C-Suite Blind Spot

- How AI and automation oversight protected brand representation
- How investment contributed to resilience for future disruptions

Next-Year Commitments

Priority Initiatives:

- Three to five funded initiatives with timelines

Capability Building:

- Training and talent plans supporting resilience and skill continuity

Technology & Data:

- Platform improvements enabling automation, accuracy, and scalability

Target Maturity Gains:

- Where ratings will improve next year — and how success will be measured

Approval and Publication

Approved by:

- Executive Sponsor
- Senior SEO/Visibility Leader
- Chief Risk or Compliance Representative

Publication:

- Included in annual business review
- Shared selectively with investors and regulators (as appropriate)

- Internal version visible to all employees

When discoverability is governed transparently and resiliently, trust becomes a proven outcome — not an assumption.

INDEX

www.ingramcontent.com/pod-product-compliance
Lightning Source LLC
Chambersburg PA
CBHW080447030726
47592CB00011B/3004